THE CIVIL WAR

VISUAL ENCYCLOPEDIA

Senior Editor Rupa Rao
Project Art Editor Heena Sharma
Project Editors Kathakali Banerjee, Bharti Bedi
Art Editor Tanisha Mandal
Assistant Editor Sukriti Kapoor
US Editor Kayla Dugger
US Executive Editor Lori Cates Hand
Senior Picture Researcher Surya Sankash Sarangi
Picture Research Manager Taiyaba Khatoon
Managing Editor Kingshuk Ghoshal
Managing Art Editor Govind Mittal
Senior DTP Designer Shanker Prasad
DTP Designer Ashok Kumar
Pre-production Manager Balwant Singh
Production Manager Pankaj Sharma
Production Editor Gillian Reid
Senior Production Controller Meskerem Berhane
Jacket Designer Tanya Mehrotra
DK India Editorial Head Glenda Fernandes
DK India Design Head Malavika Talukder
Jacket Design Development Manager Sophia MTT
Publisher Andrew Macintyre
Associate Publishing Director Liz Wheeler
Art Director Karen Self
Publishing Director Jonathan Metcalf

Written by Philip Parker
Consultants Robert Zeller, Dr. Scott Hancock
US Authenticity Reader De'Ondria Hudson
Smithsonian Consultant Jennifer L. Jones,
Curator/Project Director, Military History,
National Museum of American History

First American Edition, 2021
Published in the United States by DK Publishing
1745 Broadway, 20th Floor, New York, NY 10019

A catalog record for this book is available
from the Library of Congress.
ISBN 978-0-7440-2845-4

DK books are available at special discounts
when purchased in bulk for sales promotions,
premiums, fund-raising, or educational use.
For details, contact: DK Publishing Special Markets,
1745 Broadway, 20th Floor, New York, NY 10019
SpecialSales@dk.com

Printed and bound in China

For the curious
www.dk.com

Smithsonian

Established in 1846, the Smithsonian is the
world's largest museum and research
complex, dedicated to public education,
national service, and scholarship in the arts,
sciences, and history. It includes 21 museums
and galleries and the National Zoological
Park. The total number of artifacts, works of
art, and specimens in the Smithsonian's
collection is estimated at 155.5 million.

MIX
Paper | Supporting
responsible forestry
FSC™ C018179

This book was made with
Forest Stewardship Council™
certified paper – one small step
in DK's commitment to a
sustainable future.
**For more information go to
www.dk.com/our-green-pledge**

DK SMITHSONIAN ✳

THE CIVIL WAR

VISUAL ENCYCLOPEDIA

CONTENTS

CHAPTER 3
★ ★ ★ ★ ★ ★ ★ ★ ★ ★ ★ ★ ★ ★ ★ ★ ★ ★ ★
AFTER THE WAR

CHAPTER 4
★ ★ ★ ★ ★ ★ ★ ★ ★ ★ ★ ★
REFERENCE
SECTION

Map of continental USA in 1861

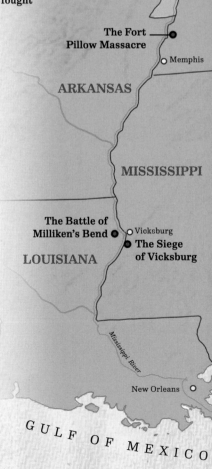

The War's Eastern Theater, the area
in which most battles were fought

THE CIVIL WAR

**THE BLOODIEST CONFLICT IN US HISTORY, THE
CIVIL WAR KILLED ALMOST 620,000 SOLDIERS
IN FOUR YEARS OF FIGHTING THAT BEGAN IN 1861.**

It erupted over the issue of slavery, which had a lot of support
in the South. Eleven Southern states broke away to form the
independent country of the Confederate States of America,
leading to War with the twenty Northern states that remained in
the Union. Five border states that allowed slavery also chose to
remain in the Union. The Confederates held their own against
the Union armies after the first major battle at Bull Run until the
tide began to turn at Gettysburg in 1863. After more than 10,500
skirmishes and battles in the War, the Confederacy finally
surrendered in 1865, leading to the restoration of the Union
and the abolition of slavery. As the two sides tried to function
as one again, there were ups and downs. The realities of
freedom for former enslaved African Americans were harsh,
and the social unrest that followed led to scars that have lasted.

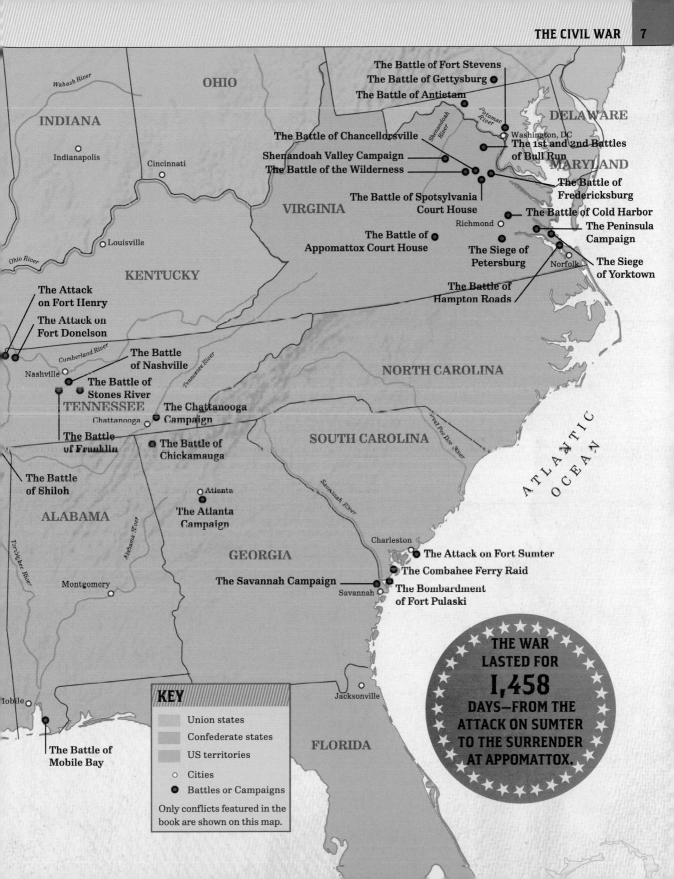

OHIO

Wabash River

INDIANA

Indianapolis

Cincinnati

The Battle of Fort Stevens
The Battle of Gettysburg
The Battle of Antietam

Potomac River

DELAWARE

Shenandoah River

Washington, DC

The Battle of Chancellorsville

Shenandoah Valley Campaign

The Battle of the Wilderness

The 1st and 2nd Battles
of Bull Run

MARYLAND

The Battle of
Fredericksburg

VIRGINIA

The Battle of Spotsylvania
Court House

The Battle of Cold Harbor

Richmond

The Peninsula
Campaign

Louisville

The Battle of
Appomattox Court House

The Siege of
Petersburg

The Siege
of Yorktown

Norfolk

Ohio River

KENTUCKY

The Battle of
Hampton Roads

The Attack
on Fort Henry

The Attack on
Fort Donelson

Cumberland River

The Battle
of Nashville

NORTH CAROLINA

Nashville

Tennessee River

The Battle of
Stones River

TENNESSEE

The Chattanooga
Campaign

Great Pee Dee River

Chattanooga

SOUTH CAROLINA

The Battle
of Franklin

The Battle of
Chickamauga

The Battle
of Shiloh

Savannah River

Atlanta

ALABAMA

The Atlanta
Campaign

Charleston

Alabama River

GEORGIA

The Attack on Fort Sumter

The Combahee Ferry Raid

Montgomery

The Savannah Campaign

Tombigbee River

Savannah

The Bombardment
of Fort Pulaski

Jacksonville

Mobile

ATLANTIC OCEAN

FLORIDA

The Battle of
Mobile Bay

KEY

Union states
Confederate states
US territories
○ Cities
● Battles or Campaigns

Only conflicts featured in the
book are shown on this map.

**THE WAR
LASTED FOR
1,458
DAYS—FROM THE
ATTACK ON SUMTER
TO THE SURRENDER
AT APPOMATTOX.**

THE COURSE OF
THE WAR

THE CIVIL WAR BROKE OUT IN 1861, AFTER 40 YEARS OF ATTEMPTS TO PREVENT THE ISSUE OF SLAVERY FROM TEARING THE COUNTRY APART.

Over the next four years, the Union and Confederacy fought more than 50 major battles, including Antietam and Gettysburg. The Confederate surrender in 1865 led to the abolition of slavery and a 12-year period of Reconstruction as attempts were made to reform the politics of the South.

1850–1860: BEFORE THE WAR »

THE COMPROMISE OF 1850
September 9–20, 1850
California enters the Union as a free state.

Congressional supporters of the Compromise of 1850

« 1861–1865: THE WAR

THE PENINSULA CAMPAIGN
April 4–July 1, 1862
Union commander George McClellan lands a large force on the Virginia Peninsula, but a delay in attacking the Confederate forces results in failure.

THE FIRST BATTLE OF BULL RUN
July 21, 1861
Union forces receive an early shock near Washington, DC, and are forced to retreat.

THE CONFEDERACY FORMS
February 8, 1861
The Confederate States of America forms. It includes seven Southern states, with four more joining later.

THE BATTLE OF ANTIETAM
September 17, 1862
Union and Confederate forces fight to a bloody draw.

THE ATTACK ON FORT SUMTER
April 12, 1861
Confederate forces open fire on the Union-held Fort Sumter in South Carolina.

THE EMANCIPATION PROCLAMATION
January 1, 1863
President Lincoln issues an edict declaring enslaved people free in the South.

THE GETTYSBURG ADDRESS
November 19, 1863
Lincoln delivers one of his most famous speeches to dedicate the Gettysburg National Cemetery in Gettysburg, Pennsylvania.

THE FALL OF RICHMOND
April 3, 1865
Richmond is taken by Union forces after the Confederates evacuate it.

THE BATTLE OF GETTYSBURG
July 1–3, 1863
Confederate General Lee's invasion of the North ends in disaster for the Confederacy.

SHERMAN'S MARCH TO THE SEA
November 15–December 10, 1864
Union General Sherman marches from Atlanta to Savannah with his men as they destroy food supplies and railroad lines in Georgia.

UNCLE TOM'S CABIN

March 20, 1852
Uncle Tom's Cabin, an antislavery novel written by abolitionist Harriet Beecher Stowe, is published.

THE KANSAS-NEBRASKA ACT

May 30, 1854
Congress passes this Act, letting two new territories—Kansas and Nebraska—decide whether to allow slavery when they become states.

BLEEDING KANSAS

May 21, 1856
Members of a proslavery group attack and ransack Lawrence, Kansas.

THE UNION BREAKS

December 20, 1860
South Carolina becomes the first state to secede, or break away, from the Union.

THE RAID ON HARPERS FERRY

October 16–18, 1859
Abolitionist John Brown attacks the federal armory at Harpers Ferry but fails to seize it.

THE DRED SCOTT DECISION

March 6, 1857
The Supreme Court rules against Dred Scott's bid for freedom, saying that African American people are not citizens of the US.

LINCOLN BECOMES PRESIDENT

November 6, 1860
Republican Abraham Lincoln is elected 16th president of the US.

John Brown

Monument to Dred Scott and his wife

1866 ONWARD: AFTER THE WAR »

LINCOLN KILLED

April 14, 1865
Confederate sympathizer John Wilkes Booth fatally shoots Lincoln, who dies early the next morning.

LEE SURRENDERS

April 9, 1865
Lee surrenders his army to Union General Ulysses S. Grant at Appomattox Court House. The remaining Confederate forces surrender soon afterward.

THE THIRTEENTH AMENDMENT

December 6, 1865
The 13th Amendment becomes law after 27 states approve it. Slavery is abolished as a result.

JUNETEENTH

June 19, 1865
On this day, Union forces liberating Galveston, Texas, declare the local enslaved people free. Many African American communities celebrate this day as Juneteenth.

THE FIRST RECONSTRUCTION ACT

March 2, 1867
Congress passes a measure that requires former Confederate states to guarantee the voting rights of African American men in order to be readmitted into the Union.

THE FIFTEENTH AMENDMENT

February 3, 1870
African American men are granted the right to vote.

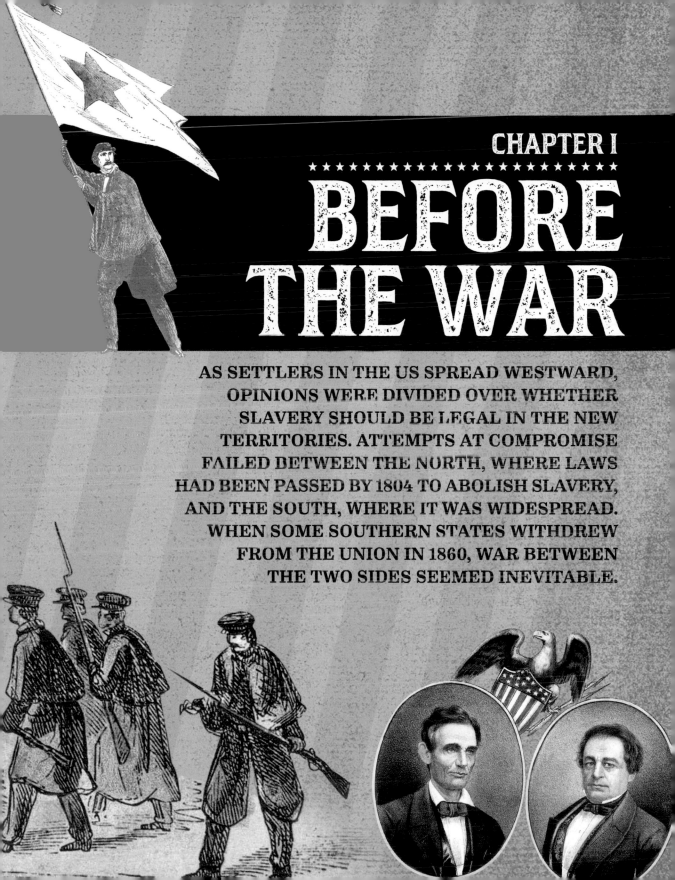

CHAPTER I

★★★★★★★★★★★★★★★★★★★★★★★★

BEFORE THE WAR

AS SETTLERS IN THE US SPREAD WESTWARD, OPINIONS WERE DIVIDED OVER WHETHER SLAVERY SHOULD BE LEGAL IN THE NEW TERRITORIES. ATTEMPTS AT COMPROMISE FAILED BETWEEN THE NORTH, WHERE LAWS HAD BEEN PASSED BY 1804 TO ABOLISH SLAVERY, AND THE SOUTH, WHERE IT WAS WIDESPREAD. WHEN SOME SOUTHERN STATES WITHDREW FROM THE UNION IN 1860, WAR BETWEEN THE TWO SIDES SEEMED INEVITABLE.

WHAT CAUSED THE WAR?

BY THE 1850s, THE INTERESTS OF THE SOUTHERN AND NORTHERN STATES HAD GROWN APART CONSIDERABLY.

Part of this was economic, with the industrialized North growing more reliant on immigrant labor, while the South depended on agriculture and slave labor. Slavery proved the key point of difference. It had existed in the North, but by the early 1800s was rare, and played no important economic or political role. The South's use of enslaved African American labor to operate its agricultural plantations and its insistence that this practice not be curbed caused a series of political crises. The final one of these in 1860–1861 sparked the Civil War.

SLAVERY

By the mid-19th century, slave labor shipped from Africa had become concentrated in the Southern states. As the US expanded westward, arguments erupted over whether slavery should be allowed in these new territories.

An iron collar with bells could be used to keep track of enslaved people likely to run away.

Enslaved laborers pick cotton in the fields.

An African American man in shackles

THE SOUTHERN ECONOMY

The South's mainly rural economy depended heavily on the export of cotton produced on big plantations by slave labor. Machinery was largely limited to Eli Whitney's cotton gin.

A POLITICAL DIVIDE

In 1850, a law forced citizens to help in returning escaped enslaved people to their slaveholders, causing a backlash in the North. Then, in 1854, the Kansas-Nebraska Act overturned the Missouri Compromise (see page 17) by allowing territories to decide for themselves whether to allow slavery. This led to political violence between pro- and antislavery groups in Kansas.

100 DOLLARS REWARD!

Ranaway from the subscriber on the 27th of July, my Black Woman, named

EMILY,

Seventeen years of age, well grown, black color, has a whining voice. She took with her one dark calico and one blue and white dress, a red corded gingham bonnet; a white striped shawl and slippers. I will pay the above reward if taken near the Ohio river on the Kentucky side, or THREE HUNDRED DOLLARS, if taken in the State of Ohio, and delivered to me near Lewisburg, Mason County, Ky.   THO'S. H. WILLIAMS.
August 4, 1853.

Hannibal Hamlin, Lincoln's running mate, became vice president.

Lincoln campaign button

Poster from 1853 offering a reward for an escaped enslaved person

LINCOLN'S ELECTION

Opponents of slavery founded the Republican Party in 1854 to oppose the Kansas-Nebraska Act. Their 1860 presidential nominee Abraham Lincoln won against rival Democratic candidates who split the opposition vote. Although Lincoln's position on slavery was comparatively moderate, Southern politicians feared the election of a Republican president meant further restrictions would be placed on it.

THE UNION IS BROKEN

After Lincoln became president, 11 Southern states broke away from the Union one by one, beginning with South Carolina in December 1860. In February 1861, seven of these formed the Confederate States of America, later to be joined by four more. By April 1861, as the Confederacy threatened to occupy federal military installations in the South, war seemed inevitable. This print shows Jefferson Davis being sworn in as president of the Confederacy.

THE NORTH-SOUTH
DIVIDE

THE INDUSTRIAL REVOLUTION AFFECTED THE NORTHERN AND SOUTHERN STATES DIFFERENTLY.

Inventions such as the steam engine powered new textile factories in the North, attracting people seeking jobs to growing cities such as Boston and New York. The need for workers increased immigration, particularly from European countries. Transportation links improved with the building of new railroads and the opening of the Erie Canal to New York City. Meanwhile, in the South, the invention of the cotton gin by Eli Whitney in 1793 sped cotton production, increasing the South's dependence on growing cotton.

These differences caused tensions. In 1828, Congress passed a tariff, setting a tax on imports of manufactured goods from Europe to protect the industries in the North. White southerners thought this was unfair because it meant they had to pay more for raw materials and goods bought from abroad and that they would face a decline in their profits, which increasingly depended on slave labor.

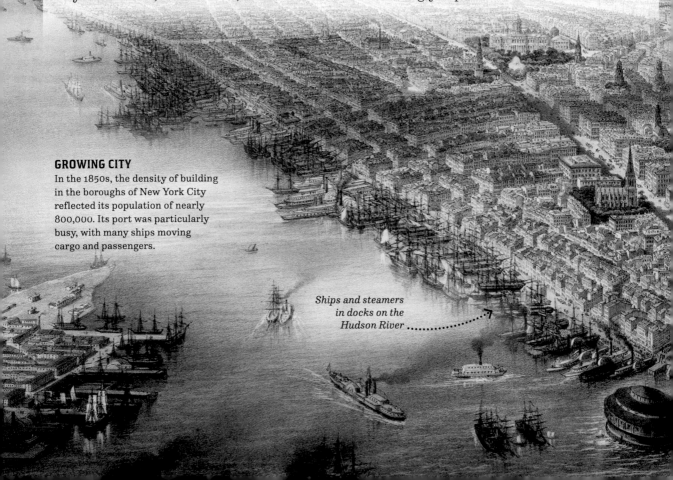

GROWING CITY
In the 1850s, the density of building in the boroughs of New York City reflected its population of nearly 800,000. Its port was particularly busy, with many ships moving cargo and passengers.

Ships and steamers in docks on the Hudson River ....

AGRICULTURAL SOUTH

The South's economy depended on the four million enslaved people who labored on sugar, rice, tobacco, and cotton plantations. Families of African Americans, including young children, were treated as property by the white plantation owners and made to work long hours in the fields without wages. This produced huge profits for the owners.

INDUSTRIAL NORTH

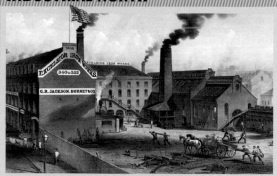

Although the textile industry was vital to its economy, the North grew rich because of the wide range of goods manufactured there, which serviced a growing middle class. New York City had many factories, such as the Excelsior Iron Works on the East River, which specialized in cast iron for railings and iron frames.

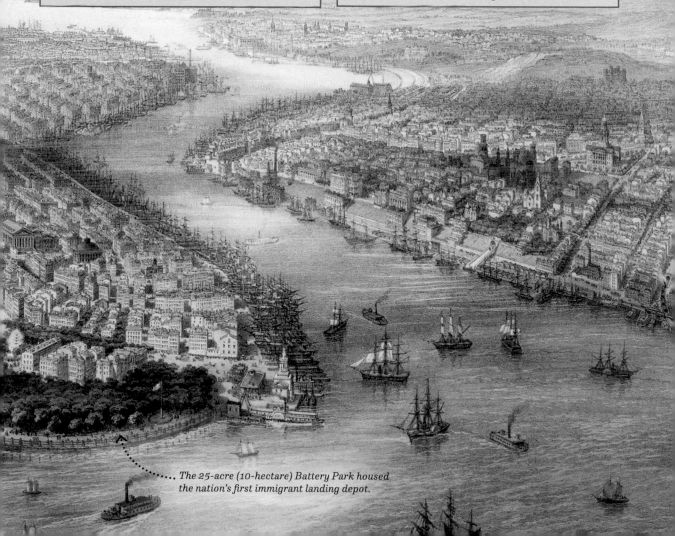

The 25-acre (10-hectare) Battery Park housed the nation's first immigrant landing depot.

FREE AND SLAVE
STATES

THE CONSTITUTION OF THE US LEFT DECISIONS ON SLAVERY TO INDIVIDUAL STATES.

As the country expanded, proslavery groups argued that slavery should be allowed in new states created from the territories acquired by the Louisiana Purchase of 1803. This debate continued with a war with Mexico in 1846–1848 that won the US more territory. The Compromise of 1850 allowed some of these areas (Utah and New Mexico) to decide for themselves but admitted California as a free state. Congress also introduced a revised Fugitive Slave Act in 1850, which required citizens to help capture enslaved people who had escaped. Many northerners reacted strongly against this law.

In 1854, tensions rose again when the Kansas-Nebraska Act let territories decide if they wanted to enter the Union as free or slave states. Pro- and antislavery groups each feared the other side would become dominant in Congress, and violence erupted, particularly in Kansas.

KANSAS BLEEDS
Proslavery "Border Ruffians"—called so because they came over the border from Missouri—and antislavery "Free Staters" fight in Kansas. These conflicts escalated from 1855 to 1859, and the state came to be called "Bleeding Kansas."

MISSOURI COMPROMISE

The Missouri Compromise was passed in 1820 to try to preserve the balance between free and slave states in Congress. It prohibited slavery in territory acquired by the Louisiana Purchase north of the 36° 30' latitude line but allowed it south of that line.

An 1820 letter by a US senator discussing the Compromise

SLAVERY

ABOUT 388,000 AFRICANS WERE TRANSPORTED TO NORTH AMERICA FROM 1619 TO 1860 TO BE ENSLAVED.

Many were put to work on the plantations that flourished throughout the South, especially after the invention of the cotton gin in 1793. There, they toiled under often-oppressive slaveholders.

While laws against slavery had been passed in the North by 1804, and the importation of enslaved people was made illegal in 1808, the South had become economically dependent on slavery. By 1860, it had nearly 4 million enslaved workers. Enslaved people had little ability to resist; some did so passively by working slowly, while others escaped, and a few—including Nat Turner—revolted. Turner recruited 75 enslaved men, his group killing around 60 white people in 1831, before local militia put the revolt down.

ON A PLANTATION

Many plantation owners held large numbers of enslaved African American people. About 100 of them can be seen in this 1862 photograph taken on a plantation near Beaufort, South Carolina.

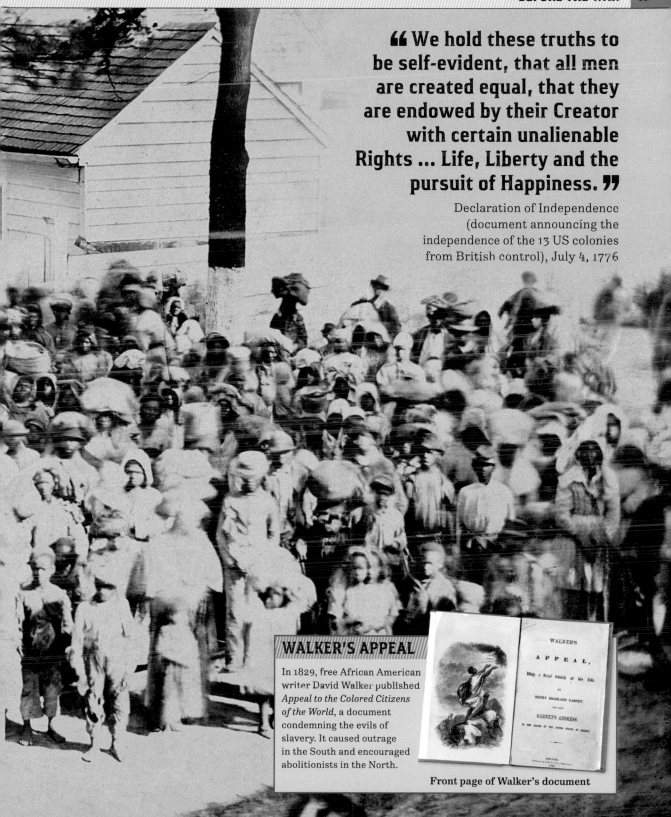

" We hold these truths to be self-evident, that all men are created equal, that they are endowed by their Creator with certain unalienable Rights ... Life, Liberty and the pursuit of Happiness. "

Declaration of Independence (document announcing the independence of the 13 US colonies from British control), July 4, 1776

WALKER'S APPEAL

In 1829, free African American writer David Walker published *Appeal to the Colored Citizens of the World*, a document condemning the evils of slavery. It caused outrage in the South and encouraged abolitionists in the North.

Front page of Walker's document

ABOLITIONISTS

By the mid-19th century, a growing number of people were calling for slavery to be made illegal. They were the abolitionists. A newspaper called *The Liberator*, founded in 1831 by abolitionist William Lloyd Garrison, acted as a rallying point for them, aided by the American Anti-Slavery Society, established in 1833. Many abolitionists were African Americans; some were born free in the North, while others escaped enslavement. In the South, the abolitionists met with ridicule or violence. In the North, that was often true, too, but they also had many who supported them.

SOJOURNER TRUTH
Born in New York City when slavery was legal, Truth escaped to become an abolitionist and women's rights activist.

JOHN BROWN
Brown attacked proslavery settlers in Kansas and tried to raise a revolt of enslaved people by raiding Harpers Ferry.

WILLIAM LLOYD GARRISON
Although a pacifist, Garrison's radical views argued for Northern separation from the slaveholding South.

SOLOMON NORTHUP
Born free, Northup was caught and enslaved for 12 years. He later became an abolitionist, wrote a memoir, and gave lectures.

SUSAN B. ANTHONY
A champion of women's suffrage (right to vote), Anthony was also an agent of the American Anti-Slavery Society.

MARY EDWARDS WALKER
A committed abolitionist, Walker served as a surgeon in the Union Army and was awarded the Medal of Honor.

EYEWITNESS: FREDERICK DOUGLASS
FREE MAN

Frederick Douglass

IN AN APPEAL TO PRESIDENT LINCOLN IN 1861, DOUGLASS ARGUED AGAINST THE GOVERNMENT'S POLICY TO TURN DOWN AFRICAN AMERICANS WHO TRIED TO ENLIST IN THE UNION ARMY, SOLELY ON ACCOUNT OF THEIR RACE.

"Unchain that Black hand!", he wrote. "We are fighting the rebels with only one hand when we should be striking with both." The Militia Act of 1862 and the Emancipation Proclamation (see page 79) in 1863 would finally allow the enlistment of African American troops to fight the Confederacy.

Frederick Douglass's brutal treatment as an enslaved person in the South before his escape in 1838 led to him becoming an abolitionist. He was also a prolific writer, and his family history notes began with Isaac and Betsy Bailey, his great-great-great grandparents, "both of them living and dying slaves."

THE SALE OF
ENSLAVED PEOPLE

**ENSLAVED BLACK PEOPLE WERE OFTEN SOLD TO
WHITE SLAVEHOLDERS AT AUCTIONS, DIRECTLY FROM
THE SHIPS THAT TRANSPORTED THEM FROM AFRICA.**

They would also be sold between plantations. At an auction, they
were paraded in front of prospective buyers, who would make
bids to buy them. The highest bidder would make the purchase.
Many of the enslaved people—including children—would
often await their turn to be sold. These sales regularly
broke up families.

    The average price of enslaved people quadrupled between
1800 and 1860 to about $1,500 as cotton production grew
and auctions—often advertised
by posters—became
more frequent.

An 1856 poster advertising
a sale of enslaved people

LIVES FOR AUCTION
Enslaved people up for sale would be
examined closely by potential white
buyers before they made their bid.

UNCLE TOM'S CABIN

THE ABOLITIONIST HARRIET BEECHER STOWE PUBLISHED HER NOVEL *UNCLE TOM'S CABIN* IN 1852.

It brought some of the harsh realities of slavery to a wider, mainly white audience who were aware of slavery but had not experienced it directly. Set against the backdrop of the Fugitive Slave Act, the book's main character Tom is sold from his plantation to a brutal slaveholder, while another, Eliza, escapes but is hunted down by a ruthless slave catcher.

The book sold 300,000 copies in its first year, infuriating proslavery politicians, who believed that the representation of enslaved African Americans in the book was unrealistic.

Seen near their cabin in this illustration are Uncle Tom, his sons Mose and Pete, his baby daughter Polly, and his wife Chloe.

UNCLE TOM'S CABIN SOLD ABOUT **2 MILLION** COPIES IN THE 1850s.

135,000 SETS, 270,000 VOLUMES SOLD.

UNCLE TOM'S CABIN

FOR SALE HERE.

AN EDITION FOR THE MILLION, COMPLETE IN 1 Vol., PRICE 37 1-2 CENTS.
" " IN GERMAN, IN 1 Vol., PRICE 50 CENTS.
" " IN 2 Vols., CLOTH, 6 PLATES, PRICE $1.50.
SUPERB ILLUSTRATED EDITION, IN 1 Vol., WITH 153 ENGRAVINGS,
PRICES FROM $2.50 TO $5.00.

The Greatest Book of the Age.

BEST-SELLING BOOK
Posters advertising *Uncle Tom's Cabin* proudly proclaimed its huge sales success. An edition in German showed how the book also appealed to New England's large German-speaking community.

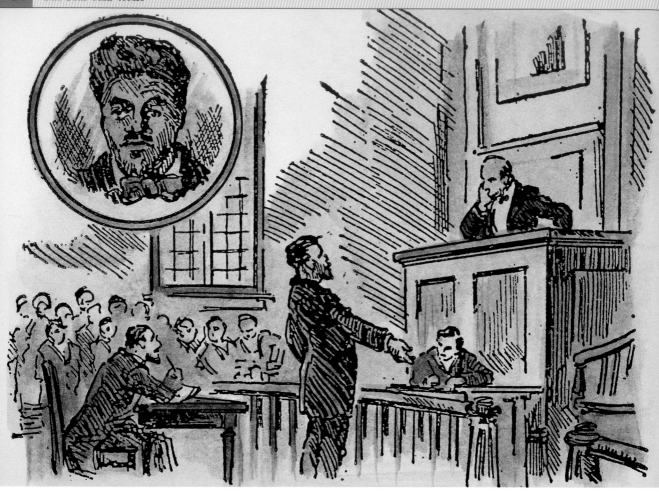

THE DRED SCOTT
DECISION

THE VERDICT
The Supreme Court Chief Justice Roger Taney
delivers the top court's decision to Dred Scott.
The Scotts were finally freed by a new slaveholder
shortly after the Supreme Court case, but Dred
Scott died the following year from tuberculosis.

**AN ENSLAVED AFRICAN AMERICAN MAN IN MISSOURI,
DRED SCOTT, SUED FOR HIS RIGHT TO FREEDOM IN 1846.**

He claimed that he had lived for several years in Wisconsin
Territory, where slavery was outlawed. In 1857, the Supreme
Court decided against him, ruling that African Americans
were not US citizens and so could not take legal action.

It also stated that Congress could not stop slavery in new
territories, effectively overturning the Missouri Compromise
(see page 17). The decision shocked the North because it
opened the way for slavery's spread to new areas.

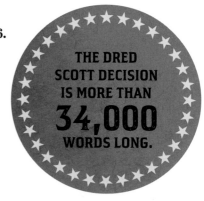

THE DRED
SCOTT DECISION
IS MORE THAN
34,000
WORDS LONG.

HARRIET TUBMAN

BORN TO AN ENSLAVED AFRICAN AMERICAN FAMILY ON A MARYLAND PLANTATION, HARRIET TUBMAN SUFFERED TERRIBLE CRUELTY.

She started working at an early age and was often beaten by white slaveholders. One of them fractured her skull with a heavy weight.

Tubman escaped and became a "conductor," or guide, in a secret network of antislavers called the "Underground Railroad" (see pages 26–27). She led more than 70 enslaved people to freedom in the North and earned the nickname "General Tubman." During the Civil War, she worked with Union forces in the South as an armed scout and spy, and later as a nurse.

> **" Slavery is the next thing to hell. "**

Harriet Tubman, 1855

A LIFE OF POVERTY
After the Civil War, Harriet Tubman lived on a property near New York City given to her by an abolitionist supporter, but she struggled with poverty until finally receiving a pension from the government in 1899.

TO FREEDOM

This view of this sculpture in Battle Creek, Michigan, shows Harriet Tubman and Underground Railroad "conductor" Erastus Hussey leading a group of escaped enslaved people to freedom. They used their knowledge of the landscape to evade pursuers.

A STATION ON THE UNDERGROUND RAILROAD

The abolitionist John Rankin's Ohio house was one of the earliest "stations" on the Underground Railroad. Rankin used lanterns to signal to escaping people that it was safe to cross the nearby Ohio River. He gave shelter to about 2,000 runaways.

The Rankin House, Ripley, Ohio

THE UNDERGROUND
RAILROAD

THE FUGITIVE SLAVE ACT OF 1793 MADE IT A LEGAL OBLIGATION TO RETURN ENSLAVED RUNAWAYS TO THEIR WHITE SLAVEHOLDERS.

This made it dangerous for those trying to escape. A network of sympathetic antislavers sprung up to help those fleeing the Southern states to freedom in the North. This was nicknamed the "Underground Railroad," with "conductors" as guides and "stationmasters" who provided safe houses. Most of the roughly 100,000 people who escaped using it came from the border states, but a new Fugitive Slave Act in 1850 made the penalties for helping them even harsher.

The declaration of secession (withdrawal from the Union) of South Carolina in 1860 listed the refusal of the Northern authorities to enforce the Fugitive Slave Act as the main reason for its action.

THE ENGINE HOUSE
US Marines force their way at bayonet point into the engine house at Harpers Ferry's federal armory, where Brown and his raiders had been trapped.

JOHN BROWN ATTACKS
HARPERS FERRY

IN THE SUMMER OF 1859, THE ABOLITIONIST JOHN BROWN MOVED TO MARYLAND, WHERE HE PLANNED A RAID ON THE FEDERAL ARMORY AT HARPERS FERRY IN VIRGINIA.

He intended to use the weapons he seized in an uprising of enslaved people whom he planned to free. When he attacked on October 16, he had just 21 followers, including five African Americans. Brown's plan failed, and he was trapped by the local militia and then arrested by the US Marines. His trial and execution attracted great publicity for the abolitionist cause.

BROWN'S TRIAL AND EXECUTION **INSPIRED** THE UNION ARMY MARCHING SONG *JOHN BROWN'S BODY.*

JEFFERSON
DAVIS

THE CONFEDERACY'S ONLY PRESIDENT, JEFFERSON DAVIS WAS A FORMER ARMY OFFICER.

He was also President Franklin Pierce's Secretary of War. His moderate views on slavery helped him win the support of states in the upper South. However, Davis quarreled with many of his generals and his vice president, promoted incompetent friends, and neglected the Western Theater (see page 114) in favor of the defense of Richmond, the Confederate capital.

FACT FILE

BORN: 1808
DIED: 1889

TERM:
1861–1865

POLITICAL PARTY:
Democratic Party
(before the War)

1853–1857: Serves as Secretary of War

1861: Selected as Confederate president

1865: Captured and imprisoned for two years before receiving presidential pardon

LEADER IN THE SOUTH
Shown here around 1860, Davis was one of the South's most experienced politicians, having served as Congressman and Senator from Mississippi.

ABRAHAM
LINCOLN

LINCOLN GREW UP IN AN INDIANA LOG CABIN AND ROSE FROM HIS HUMBLE BEGINNINGS TO BECOME A LAWYER AND FINALLY PRESIDENT.

A well-known opponent of slavery, Lincoln's election in 1860 was used by Southern radicals to argue for secession (withdrawal from the Union). He was an inspirational wartime leader and not afraid to make hard choices, such as firing the popular general George McClellan (see page 78).

Union victories helped him win reelection in 1864. His belief that slavery was unjust overrode his wish to reconcile with the South, and he called for the emancipation of enslaved people in the areas held by the Confederacy. He was assassinated (see page 137) by a Confederate sympathizer named John Wilkes Booth.

MAN WITH THE BEARD
Lincoln grew his trademark beard in 1860, after an 11-year-old girl wrote to him suggesting it would make his face look less thin, and so make more people vote for him.

FACT FILE

BORN: 1809
DIED: 1865

TERMS:
1861–1865, 1865

PARTY: Republican Party (until 1864), National Union Party (1864–1865)

1861: Calls for volunteers to defend the Union

1863: Issues Emancipation Proclamation that began to free enslaved people

1865: Assassinated by John Wilkes Booth

SLAVE POWER

THE TERM "SLAVE POWER" DENOTED THE POWER AND INFLUENCE OF SLAVEHOLDERS AND THEIR WHITE POLITICAL SUPPORTERS.

As arguments over slavery grew in the 1850s, many northerners complained that slaveholding states had an unfair influence over federal politics. They said that "slave power" politicians (or the "slavocracy") were working to spread slavery into new areas and to stop new limits being imposed on it. They pointed to the constitution's "Three-Fifths Clause," which included enslaved people in the population of a state for the purposes of calculating how many Congressmen it had, inflating the number of Southern representatives who could block antislavery measures.

An 1854 edition of Frederick Douglass's newspaper that accused "slave power" in Congress of promoting a proslavery Act

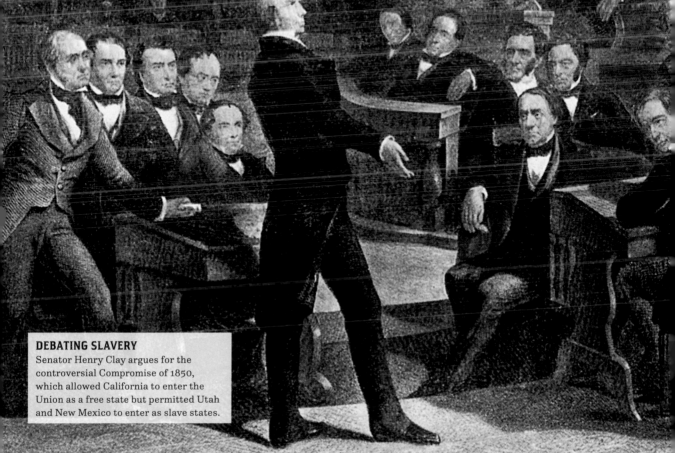

DEBATING SLAVERY
Senator Henry Clay argues for the controversial Compromise of 1850, which allowed California to enter the Union as a free state but permitted Utah and New Mexico to enter as slave states.

LINCOLN BECOMES
PRESIDENT

THE REPUBLICAN PARTY SELECTED LINCOLN AS ITS 1860 PRESIDENTIAL CANDIDATE FOR HIS LESS RADICAL VIEWS ON THE ISSUE OF SLAVERY.

Lincoln faced a divided opposition. The Democrats, broken into Northern and Southern factions, chose Stephen Douglas and John Breckinridge as their candidates. The Constitutional Union Party's John Bell appealed to many border state voters. While Lincoln's opponents split the vote in the South, he swept the North, winning with less than 40 percent of the national vote.

FIRST ADDRESS

Between Lincoln's election and his inaugural address in March 1861, seven states had seceded, but he told the crowd, "We are not enemies, but friends."

THE 1860 ELECTIONS HAD **ONE OF THE HIGHEST** TURNOUTS EVER.

THE FIVE **BORDER** STATES WERE DELAWARE, WEST VIRGINIA, MARYLAND, KENTUCKY, AND MISSOURI.

SOUTHERN STATES
LEAVE THE UNION

ABRAHAM LINCOLN'S ELECTION RAISED FEARS IN THE SOUTH THAT HE WOULD RESTRICT SLAVERY.

CONFEDERATE CELEBRATIONS

On December 20, 1860, drummers paraded and Southern supporters waved independence flags outside the hall in Charleston, where South Carolina's state convention approved the secession from the Union.

In December 1860, South Carolina's legislature voted to leave the Union. Six other states of the lower South—Alabama, Florida, Georgia, Louisiana, Mississippi, and Texas—also seceded, and on February 4, 1861, they established a country called the Confederate States of America. The upper South states—Arkansas, Tennessee, North Carolina, and Virginia—hesitated, but after the attack on Fort Sumter (see page 38), they too joined the Confederacy.

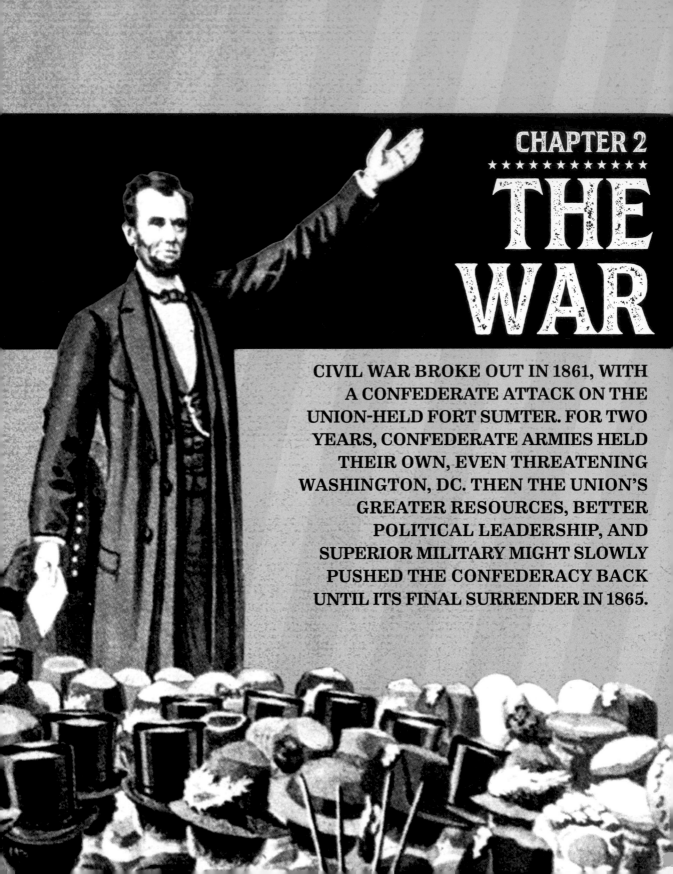

CHAPTER 2
★★★★★★★★★★★★★★
THE WAR

CIVIL WAR BROKE OUT IN 1861, WITH A CONFEDERATE ATTACK ON THE UNION-HELD FORT SUMTER. FOR TWO YEARS, CONFEDERATE ARMIES HELD THEIR OWN, EVEN THREATENING WASHINGTON, DC. THEN THE UNION'S GREATER RESOURCES, BETTER POLITICAL LEADERSHIP, AND SUPERIOR MILITARY MIGHT SLOWLY PUSHED THE CONFEDERACY BACK UNTIL ITS FINAL SURRENDER IN 1865.

THE WAR STARTS

THE BEGINNING OF THE WAR IN APRIL 1861 SET OFF A RACE BETWEEN THE UNION AND CONFEDERACY TO RECRUIT ARMIES.

With fewer resources, the Confederacy needed to win the War quickly before the North's greater industrial might and labor strength could tell. With the two sides' capital cities—the Union capital at Washington, DC, and the Confederate one at Richmond, Virginia—so close together in the east, much of the fighting took place in the area between them. The War was also fought in the West, and along the Mississippi River. The Union held off Confederate invasions in 1862 and 1863, and finally advanced through Virginia and Georgia to defeat the Confederacy.

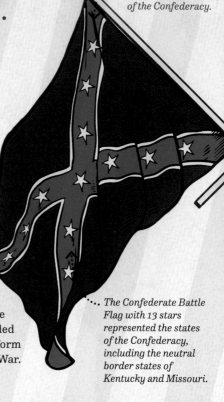

.... *This design was the most recognized symbol of the Confederacy.*

THE TWO SIDES

The War was fought between the 25 states that remained in the Union and the 11 seceded Confederate states. Both sides depended on state militias at first, then rapidly recruited regiments to form larger armies. Eventually, around 3 million soldiers fought in the War.

..... *The Confederate Battle Flag with 13 stars represented the states of the Confederacy, including the neutral border states of Kentucky and Missouri.*

WHERE WAS IT FOUGHT?

Much of the fighting took place in Virginia, Kentucky, and down the Mississippi as the Union tried to advance south. Campaigns also took place in Tennessee, and smaller ones in Kansas, Texas, and Florida. At the end of the War, Union armies marched through Alabama, Georgia, and the Carolinas.

NAMING BATTLES

Some battles had two different names. Union soldiers named them after natural features such as rivers, while Confederates found towns and villages more memorable. For instance, the battle shown above was named Shiloh by the South (after the town of Shiloh) and Pittsburg Landing by the North (for the landing on the Tennessee River).

The battlefield of Bull Run, Virginia, in 1862, about a year after the first battle .....

KEY BATTLES

Some of the main battles of the War included the First Battle of Bull Run (see right) in July 1861, where the South nearly achieved a conclusive victory to end the War. In April 1862, Union General Ulysses S. Grant's victory at Shiloh stopped the Confederacy from taking Tennessee. The Confederate defeat at Gettysburg in July 1863 ended the South's last real chance to defeat the North.

The flag of the United States (Union) with stars and stripes

Union General Ulysses S. Grant

Confederate General Robert E. Lee surrenders to the Union in 1865.

SIGNIFICANT INNOVATIONS

The Civil War saw many military advances, including the use of longer-range rifled guns, the telegraph for communication, and hot air balloons for aerial reconnaissance. At sea, heavily armored ironclads fought and naval mines sank ships. In medicine, the use of anesthetics, organized ambulance corps, and quinine against yellow fever saved many lives. Shown below is an ambulance drill by a Union medical unit.

WHY DID THE UNION WIN?

With 70 percent of the prewar population and 97 percent of the arms manufacturing capacity, the North had an unmatched advantage. Although it won battles, the South lost men that it found hard to replace and had to hope for a decisive victory that never came.

IN FLAMES
Shelling by shore-based Confederate cannons set Fort Sumter ablaze. Anderson's men were forced to lie on the ground to avoid inhaling the smoke.

The fires that broke out threatened to detonate the fort's gunpowder store.

Confederate cannons fired around 3,000 shells at Fort Sumter.

Pierre Gustave
Toutant Beauregard

THE ATTACK ON
FORT SUMTER

AS STATES SECEDED IN EARLY 1861, CONFEDERATE MILITIAS SEIZED STRATEGIC COASTAL FORTS.

Fort Sumter in Charleston Harbor remained in Union hands, garrisoned by Major Robert Anderson. The Confederates tried to starve him out by blocking supplies, but Lincoln refused to allow the fort's evacuation. On April 12, Confederate Brigadier General P. G. T. Beauregard ordered his artillery to open fire on Sumter, and after 34 hours of bombardment, Anderson surrendered. This clash marked the start of the Civil War.

FACT FILE

LOCATION:
Charleston, South Carolina

DATE:
April 12–13, 1861

WHO WON:
Confederacy

CASUALTIES: Union 0; Confederacy 0

WEST POINT
MILITARY ACADEMY

THE US MILITARY ACADEMY AT WEST POINT TRAINED MANY OFFICERS WHO KNEW EACH OTHER AND WOULD FIGHT ONE ANOTHER IN THE CIVIL WAR.

Founded in 1802, the academy was the common training ground for generations of army officers educated in the same military traditions. Union Generals William T. Sherman, George H. Thomas, George B. McClellan, and Ulysses S. Grant were all West Point graduates. Other well-known officers who studied there and would later resign their federal commissions to join the Confederate Army included Generals Robert E. Lee, Thomas "Stonewall" Jackson, and J. E. B. Stuart.

More than 500 West Point graduates had fought together against a common enemy in the Mexican-American War (1846–1848). This list included Confederate Generals Lee, Jackson, and Stuart and Union Generals McClellan and Grant.

COMRADES IN ARMS
In this picture from the 1850s, cadets of the West Point Military Academy stand together in front of one of the academy's buildings. Union General George B. McClellan and Confederate General Thomas Jackson belonged to the academy's class of 1846.

CIVIL WAR FLAGS

FLAGS WERE AN IMPORTANT POLITICAL SYMBOL FOR BOTH SIDES.

For the Union, the Stars and Stripes flag bore stars for all the states and symbolized the hope for a reunited country. One of the first acts of the Confederate Congress in January 1861 was to agree on a flag. The Confederacy had three versions by the War's end, including the "Blood-Stained Banner," introduced in 1865, which added a horizontal red bar to the "Stainless Banner." On both sides, armies, navies, and individual regiments had their own flags, which they bore proudly into battle. The flags also helped them recognize friendly troops.

CONFEDERATE FLAGS

The first Confederate flag resembled the Union's Stars and Stripes. A second version with a diagonal cross and stripes, nicknamed the "Stainless Banner," featured 13 stars, including for Kentucky and Missouri, even though they did not secede.

UNION FLAGS

The Union continued to use the prewar Stars and Stripes, with a 33-star version at the start of the War. Toward the end, a 36-star flag was introduced after the admission of Kansas, West Virginia, and Nevada as states.

The Abolitionist flag, with stars only for the free states

Stars and Stripes, with 33 stars for the states at the start of the War

The most recognized symbol of the Confederacy, the Battle Flag was introduced in November 1861 to avoid confusing the Confederacy's first flag (bottom left) with that of the Union.

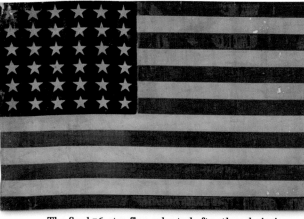

The final 36-star flag, adopted after the admission of Nevada in October 1864

Stars and Bars, the first Confederate flag, with seven stars for the first seceding states

Stainless Banner, the second flag, adopted in May 1863

Name of the recruiting regiment ....

FOURTH REGIMENT
NEW HAMPSHIRE

DOWN WITH THE REBELLION.

VOLUNTEERS.

ABLE BODIED MEN WANTED
FOR THE FOURTH REGIMENT.

The subscribers having been appointed Recruiting Officers, will open a Recruiting Office at

Where they will enlist all who would like to rally around the OLD STARS AND STRIPES, the emblem of America's Freedom.

$10 BOUNTY WILL BE ALLOWED!

Regular Army pay and Rations to commence on taking the oath.

Lieut. J. M. CLOUGH,
Sergt. W. B. ROWE.

Sept. 1861.

Fogg, Hadley & Co., Printers, Concord.

> **❝ I hereby do call forth the militia of several states of the Union, to the aggregate number of 75,000 ... ❞**
>
> President Lincoln's proclamation calling for militia volunteers, April 15, 1861

Cash bonus offered to recruits ....

CALLING FOR VOLUNTEERS
This 1861 poster called for volunteers for the Fourth New Hampshire Regiment, one of many local units recruited for the Union. The $10 bounty it offered was a way to encourage recruits with a financial incentive to get them to enlist.

RECRUITING
SOLDIERS

EARLY IN THE WAR, BOTH THE UNION AND THE CONFEDERACY NEEDED TO RECRUIT TROOPS RAPIDLY.

In March 1861, the Confederate Congress called for 100,000 volunteers, with most of its forces drawn from state militias. In April, President Lincoln asked for 75,000 volunteers and, by 1862, more than 700,000 men had joined the Union Army. Many prewar army officers, such as Robert E. Lee, joined the Confederacy, so finding enough officers for the Union Army was difficult at first.

EARLY IN THE WAR, THE UNION ARMY REFUSED TO ENLIST **AFRICAN AMERICAN** VOLUNTEERS.

THE FIRST BATTLE OF
BULL RUN

THE CONFEDERACY CALLED THIS MAJOR LAND CONFLICT THE FIRST BATTLE OF MANASSAS.

In July 1861, General Irwin McDowell's Union troops attacked the important railroad junction at Manassas in Virginia. At first, they pushed back Confederate General P. G. T. Beauregard's forces, but reinforcements reached the Confederate Army. A stubborn resistance by General Thomas Jackson on Henry Hill gave the Confederates time to counterattack, and the Union Army fled back to Washington, DC. The First Battle of Bull Run was an enormous victory for the Confederacy.

FACT FILE

 LOCATION:
Bull Run/Manassas, Virginia

 DATE:
July 21, 1861

 WHO WON:
Confederacy

 CASUALTIES: Union 2,896; Confederacy 1,982

FORCING A RETREAT

J. E. B. Stuart leads the charge of the 1st Virginia Cavalry at Bull Run. His foiling of Union infantry advances contributed to Beauregard's victory.

J. E. B. Stuart

THOMAS J. "STONEWALL"
JACKSON

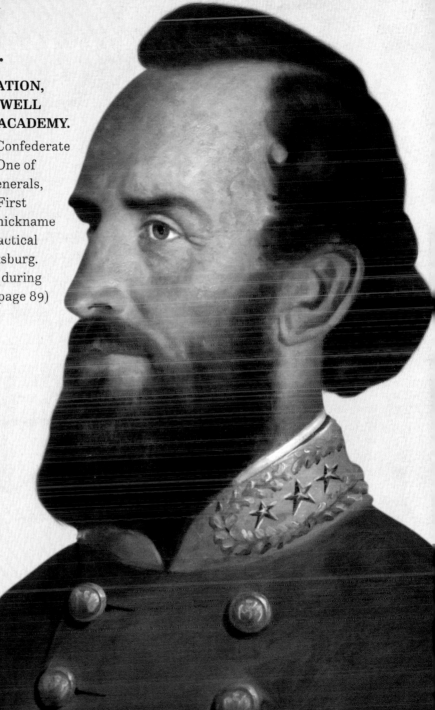

SHY AND WITH LITTLE EDUCATION, JACKSON STILL GRADUATED WELL FROM WEST POINT MILITARY ACADEMY.

A native of Virginia, he joined the Confederate forces and was quickly promoted. One of the Confederacy's most brilliant generals, Jackson's stubborn defense in the First Battle of Bull Run earned him the nickname "Stonewall." He won fame for his tactical defense at Antietam and Fredericksburg. An accidental shot by his own side during the Battle of Chancellorsville (see page 89) led to his death.

FACT FILE

 BORN: 1824
DIED: 1863

 RANK:
Major General

 ARMY: Army of Northern Virginia, Confederacy

 1861: Wins nickname "Stonewall" at Bull Run

1862: Takes major role in Fredericksburg victory

1863: Killed by friendly fire at Chancellorsville

DISTINGUISHED LEADER
This 1864 portrait of Jackson was painted to commemorate him the year after his death. His uniform bears the three stars seen on any General-rank officer in the Confederacy.

EYEWITNESS: CHARLES WILLIAM DUSTAN
UNION SOLDIER

IN A LETTER TO HIS MOTHER, CAPTAIN CHARLES WILLIAM DUSTAN MULLED OVER THE PROBLEMS OF MAINTAINING DISCIPLINE AMONG THE TROOPS.

"Still a few of us … do all we can to check and control the spirit that pervades the camp …," he wrote in the letter. Dustan was an officer in the 71st New York Militia Regiment. Militia soldiers were volunteers who often elected their own officers. Keeping discipline among them was hard, as they often objected to traditional army rules. Constant drilling and punishments led to arguments, and many men deserted, especially after battlefield defeats.

Charles William Dustan

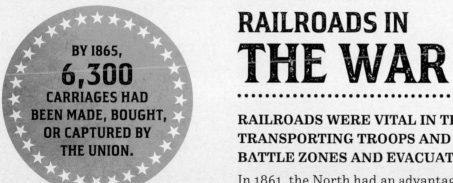

RAILROADS IN
THE WAR

RAILROADS WERE VITAL IN THE CIVIL WAR, TRANSPORTING TROOPS AND SUPPLIES TO THE BATTLE ZONES AND EVACUATING CASUALTIES.

In 1861, the North had an advantage, with about 21,000 miles (34,000 km) of track, compared to the Confederacy's 8,700 miles (14,000 km). The Confederates at first used their railroads well, transporting General Joseph Johnston's reinforcements to win at the First Battle of Bull Run (see page 42), but the loss of key junctions by 1864 and better Union coordination allowed the North to gain the upper hand.

QUICK TRANSPORTATION
Following the Battle of Gaines' Mill, 1862, injured Union soldiers were carried aboard flatbed railroad cars to nearby field hospitals. Use of the railroads allowed wounded soldiers to be transported far more rapidly for treatment.

THE ANACONDA PLAN

This cartoon map by J. B. Elliott of Cincinnati, Ohio, portrays Scott's blockade plan as an anaconda—a snake that squeezes its prey to death—wrapping itself around the Confederacy. It uses some instances of offensive language and caricatures as a way of ridiculing Southern attitudes toward slavery.

This text refers to the area set aside by the federal government for the relocation and settlement of American Indian tribes. This eventually became the state of Oklahoma.

A militiaman is shown shooting at enslaved people escaping in Texas. The $1,000 cost here refers to the average price of an enslaved person at an auction in the 1860s.

Enslaved people in Louisiana can be seen lying atop bales of cotton that can no longer be shipped because of the blockade, as hoped by the North.

The text for Mississippi uses the term "massa," playing on a stereotype of how enslaved people supposedly referred to slaveholders.

An Alabama man is shown protesting that the Confederacy has moved its capitol—the seat of its Congress—from Montgomery, Alabama, to Richmond, Virginia.

UNION
BLOCKADE

NEITHER UNION NOR CONFEDERACY WERE PREPARED FOR A LONG WAR, BUT AFTER BULL RUN, IT BECAME CLEAR THEY WOULD FIGHT ONE.

Although the South did not have to defend long lines of supply, it had few factories and had to import weapons from abroad.

Union general-in-chief Winfield Scott—a veteran of the War of 1812 against Britain and the Mexican-American War (1846–1848)—devised the "Anaconda Plan." It was a strategy to strangle the Confederacy by using the Union Navy to blockade its ports and stop supplies from getting through. Scott hoped the plan would make a land campaign unnecessary. By the end of the War, the Confederate authorities struggled to import enough to keep their armies supplied.

Escaped enslaved people, known as "contrabands," are shown heading across the border toward freedom in the North.

BLOCKADE RUNNERS

The Confederacy used steamers and other small, light vessels as blockade runners to escape the Union blockade, trying to sail to and from Southern ports. The Union Navy captured 1,500 blockade runners, but even in 1864, two-thirds of them got through, carrying guns, medicine, clothing, and tea to the Confederacy.

THE ARMED FORCES

AT THE START OF THE CIVIL WAR, THE US ARMY HAD ONLY 18,000 MEN, MOSTLY POSTED IN THE FAR WEST.

Both the Union and Confederacy had to raise volunteer regiments rapidly, leading to chaotic military structures. The new regiments, each around 2,000-strong, were given a designation for their state of origin and a number (such as the 54th Massachusetts). Around five regiments would be organized into a brigade. In the Union Army, three brigades made up a division, which included cavalry and infantry regiments, as well as artillery batteries. Three divisions formed an army corps, and several corps made army groups, such as the Union Army of the Potomac, or even the Confederate Army of Northern Virginia. The Union inherited most of the Federal Navy, but the Confederacy had to either capture or build ships.

CAVALRY CAMP

Fort Harrison was part of the Confederate defenses of Richmond, but it was overrun by Union troops in September 1864. Renamed Fort Burnham, it became the camp of the 5th Pennsylvania Cavalry—part of General Benjamin F. Butler's Army of the James, which fought in the Petersburg Campaign (see page 124).

> **❝ I have seen pictures of battles—they would all be in line, standing in a nice level field fighting … but it isn't so. ❞**
>
> Union Private William Brearley, referring to soldiers in a letter from Antietam, September 1862

THE UNION NAVY

Sailors on the Union warship USS *Mendota*

The Union Navy was organized into squadrons led by flag officers, such as the Mississippi Squadron, and smaller flotillas. At first, the Confederacy had no navy, so it used captured Union ships. Later, it built 130 vessels, including the ironclads.

CONFEDERATE
UNIFORMS

SHORTAGE OF MATERIAL SIMPLIFIED THE DESIGNS OF CONFEDERATE UNIFORMS.

Regulations in 1863 ordered the jackets to be gray, which became the main color of Southern uniforms. Officers wore long double-breasted coats, while enlisted men wore shorter waist-length jackets.

Embroidered bars on the collar indicate the rank of a lieutenant.

Battle shirt or overshirt worn in combat in place of regular uniform

Dark blue tailcoat worn by the officers of the 4th Georgia Regiment Militia

Slouch hats were often worn in place of more formal kepis.

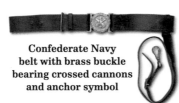

Confederate Navy belt with brass buckle bearing crossed cannons and anchor symbol

Rough leather shoes of a Confederate soldier

Kepi (military cap) of a Confederate officer, the red color indicating an artillery division

Confederate artillery officer's gray frock coat

UNION
UNIFORMS

THE WIDE RANGE OF UNIFORMS AMONG VOLUNTEER REGIMENTS IN THE UNION ARMY CAUSED CONFUSION AT THE START OF THE WAR.

Some even wore the same gray as the Confederates. By 1863, regulation dark blue uniforms had become almost universal. Colored stripes indicated branches of the Army, with badges for individual regiments.

Brass buttons

Yellow stripes denote cavalry

Jacket and sky-blue trousers of a cavalryman of the 4th Massachusetts Regiment

Artilleryman's jacket with three chevrons indicating the rank of a First Sergeant

Black leather lace-up boots for an infantryman

Knapsack of the 7th New York State Militia with leather water canteen

Fez worn by the New York Zouave (cavalry) Regiment with gold tassel

Union captain's dark blue overcoat with officer's sash tied at the left hip

FORTS HENRY AND DONELSON

TWO CONFEDERATE FORTS, HENRY AND DONELSON, BLOCKED UNION GENERAL ULYSSES S. GRANT'S ADVANCE INTO TENNESSEE IN EARLY 1862.

A bombardment by Union gunboats under Commander Andrew Foote led to Fort Henry's rapid surrender, but the Confederacy decided to defend Donelson in strength.

The garrison at Donelson commanded by Brigadier General John B. Floyd fought off an assault by Union land forces, but then a Confederate force led by Brigadier General Gideon J. Pillow decided to try to break out. The attempt, on February 15, nearly succeeded, but Pillow pulled back at the last minute and the fort fell the next day. Kentucky and Tennessee now lay open to the Union Army.

FACT FILE

LOCATION:
Forts Henry and Donelson (near Dover), Tennessee

DATE:
February 6, 1862 (Henry); February 12–16, 1862 (Donelson)

WHO WON:
Union

CASUALTIES: Union 2,733; Confederacy 13,867

THE FINAL FALL

The troops clashed at Donelson just before the fort fell to the Union Army. Around 3,000 Confederates, including General Pillow, managed to escape.

IRON ON WATER
Despite all their firepower, the iron hulls of the *Virginia* and *Monitor* were too strong for each other's shells to penetrate. But within months, both the ships had sunk—the *Virginia* by its crew to prevent its capture and the *Monitor* in a storm.

Union frigate Minnesota under attack from CSS Virginia

USS Monitor's rotating turret gun mounted on its upper hull

CSS Virginia's steel hull was 4 in (10 cm) thick.

THE CLASH OF THE
IRONCLADS

TO TRY TO BREAK THE UNION BLOCKADE, THE CONFEDERATE NAVY WELDED IRON PLATES TO THE *MERRIMACK*, A CAPTURED UNION VESSEL.

This turned it into a formidable ironclad ship, which they renamed the CSS *Virginia*. On March 9, 1862, at Hampton Roads—a meeting point for three rivers—the *Virginia* battled the USS *Monitor*, a Union ironclad with a rotating turret gun. The two fired at each other at point-blank range for hours, even as the *Virginia* tried to ram the *Monitor*. Eventually, the *Virginia*'s captain withdrew from what came to be known as the Battle of Hampton Roads—the world's first naval battle between ironclads.

FACT FILE

LOCATION:
Hampton Roads, Virginia

DATE:
March 8–9, 1862

WHO WON: No victory for either side

IRONCLADS: Union 1; Confederacy 1

THE BATTLE OF
SHILOH

ONE OF THE BLOODIEST BATTLES IN THE WAR WAS FOUGHT AT SHILOH, NEAR PITTSBURG LANDING.

In April 1862, Confederate General Albert Johnston rushed to prevent two Union armies invading Tennessee from combining. At Shiloh, near Corinth, Mississippi, he caught Union Major General Ulysses S. Grant (see page 56) by surprise. The disordered Union forces initially fell back, and only a ferocious defense prevented a Union defeat.

Overnight, Union Major General Don Carlos Buell arrived with reinforcements, and the next morning the now-superior Union side forced a Confederate retreat.

THE HORNET'S NEST
Union troops defend a sunken road in the battlefield under heavy Confederate fire. The bullets buzzing past them gave the place its nickname, "Hornet's Nest." Their stand allowed Grant to bring in reinforcements.

FACT FILE

LOCATION: Shiloh/ Pittsburg Landing, Tennessee

DATE: April 6–7, 1862

WHO WON: Union

CASUALTIES: Union 13,047; Confederacy 10,669

DRUMMER BOYS

DRUMMERS KEPT MARCHING TROOPS IN STEP AND PASSED BASIC ORDERS ON THE BATTLEFIELD.

Most drummers were very young when faced with danger on the field— Charley King was only 13 when he died of wounds at Antietam.

The most famous drummer boy, Johnny Clem, was just 9 when he joined the 22nd Michigan Union Regiment in 1861. At Shiloh in April 1862, his drum was shattered by a Confederate artillery round while he was playing it. His bravery made him a celebrity.

The horn on the cap badge indicates the infantry regiment and the letter "H" stands for the company.

STARTING YOUNG
Although young, these drummer boys were already veterans by the time this photograph was taken around 1863, having been in nine battles.

A SERGEANT AT 12, CLEM WAS THE **YOUNGEST** NONCOMMISSIONED OFFICER IN US HISTORY.

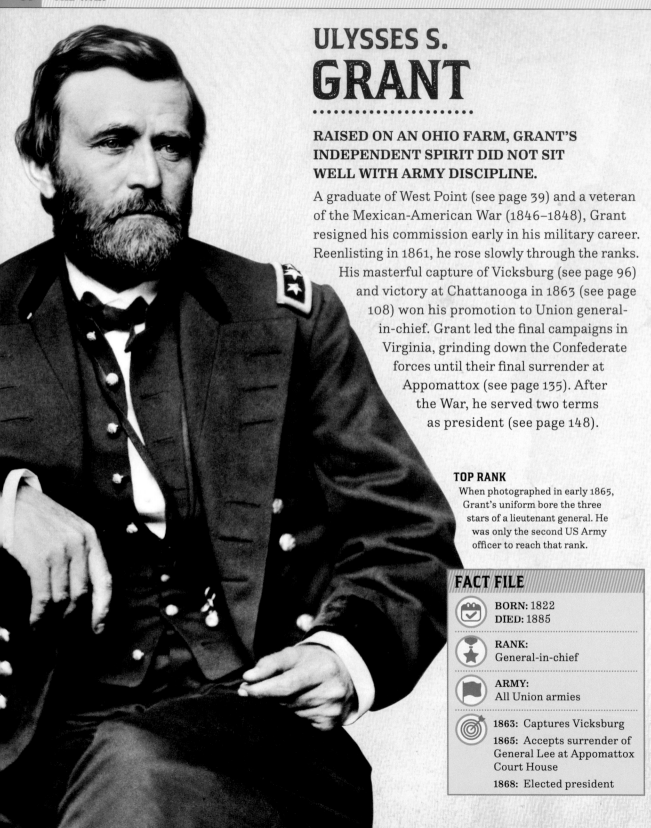

ULYSSES S.
GRANT

. . . .

RAISED ON AN OHIO FARM, GRANT'S INDEPENDENT SPIRIT DID NOT SIT WELL WITH ARMY DISCIPLINE.

A graduate of West Point (see page 39) and a veteran of the Mexican-American War (1846–1848), Grant resigned his commission early in his military career. Reenlisting in 1861, he rose slowly through the ranks. His masterful capture of Vicksburg (see page 96) and victory at Chattanooga in 1863 (see page 108) won his promotion to Union general-in-chief. Grant led the final campaigns in Virginia, grinding down the Confederate forces until their final surrender at Appomattox (see page 135). After the War, he served two terms as president (see page 148).

TOP RANK

When photographed in early 1865, Grant's uniform bore the three stars of a lieutenant general. He was only the second US Army officer to reach that rank.

FACT FILE

BORN: 1822
DIED: 1885

RANK:
General-in-chief

ARMY:
All Union armies

1863: Captures Vicksburg
1865: Accepts surrender of General Lee at Appomattox Court House
1868: Elected president

DAVID GLASGOW
FARRAGUT

AS A SOUTHERNER IN THE UNION NAVY, FARRAGUT WAS DENIED IMPORTANT COMMANDS AT FIRST.

In April 1862, this veteran of the Mexican-American War pushed a small fleet past the forts defending New Orleans, forcing the city's surrender and dealing a bitter blow to the Confederacy. After fighting in the Vicksburg Campaign (see page 96) in 1863, he led a naval assault in 1864 on Mobile, Alabama (see page 126) to capture the Confederacy's last port on the Gulf of Mexico. Although promoted to admiral, poor health prevented him from playing any further part in the War.

FACT FILE

 BORN: 1801
DIED: 1870

 RANK:
Admiral

 NAVY: West Gulf Blockading Squadron, Union

 1862: Captures New Orleans, the Confederacy's largest city

1864: Leads the Union to victory in the Battle of Mobile Bay

1866: Becomes the first US naval officer to be given the rank of admiral

COMMANDER ON DECK
Farragut (left) commanded his flagship, the USS *Hartford*. His squadron used shipboard artillery to great effect in bombarding coastal forts.

USING GUNS

AT THE START OF THE CIVIL WAR, MOST INFANTRYMEN CARRIED SINGLE-SHOT MUSKETS WITH SMOOTH BARRELS THAT WERE HARD TO RELOAD.

These guns had a range of about 87 yd (80 m) and used bullets in the shape of a round ball that fit loosely inside the barrel. Rifles, with grooves on the inside of a barrel, had four times the range, but they did not become widespread until the development of the Minié bullet, which made loading easier. From 1862, the Springfield 58-caliber rifled musket became the main infantry firearm of the Union, and the introduction of breech-loading rifles increased the rate of fire. By 1863, some Union soldiers had repeating (multishot) weapons, giving them an advantage over the Confederacy, which had little arms manufacturing capacity.

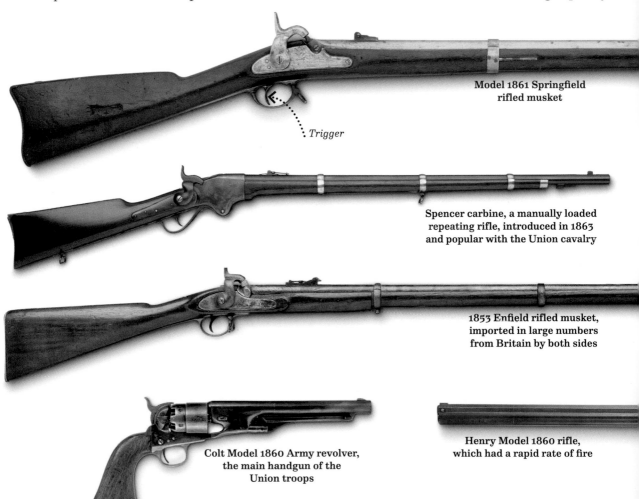

Model 1861 Springfield rifled musket

Trigger

Spencer carbine, a manually loaded repeating rifle, introduced in 1863 and popular with the Union cavalry

1853 Enfield rifled musket, imported in large numbers from Britain by both sides

Colt Model 1860 Army revolver, the main handgun of the Union troops

Henry Model 1860 rifle, which had a rapid rate of fire

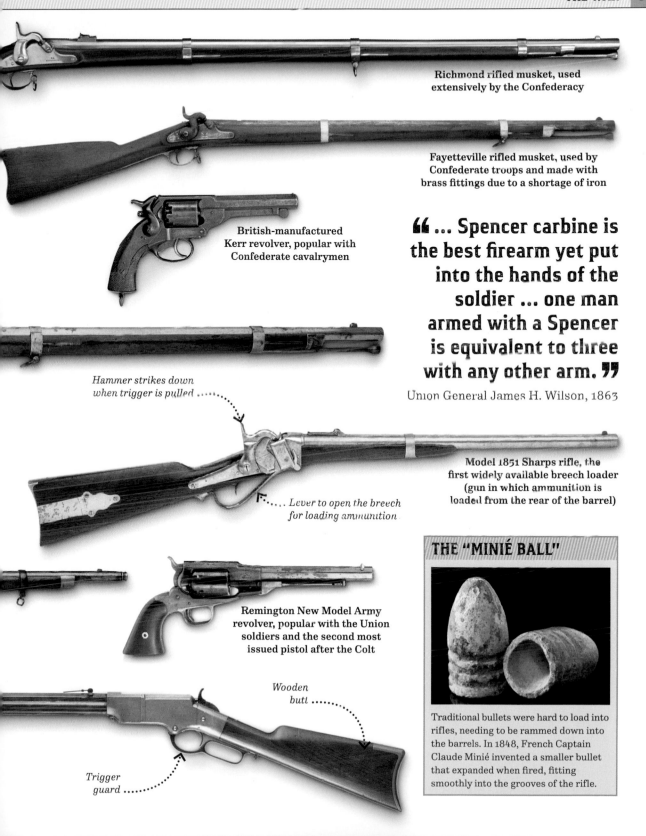

Richmond rifled musket, used extensively by the Confederacy

Fayetteville rifled musket, used by Confederate troops and made with brass fittings due to a shortage of iron

British-manufactured Kerr revolver, popular with Confederate cavalrymen

" ... Spencer carbine is the best firearm yet put into the hands of the soldier ... one man armed with a Spencer is equivalent to three with any other arm. "

Union General James H. Wilson, 1863

Hammer strikes down when trigger is pulled

Lever to open the breech for loading ammunition

Model 1851 Sharps rifle, the first widely available breech loader (gun in which ammunition is loaded from the rear of the barrel)

Remington New Model Army revolver, popular with the Union soldiers and the second most issued pistol after the Colt

Wooden butt

Trigger guard

THE "MINIÉ BALL"

Traditional bullets were hard to load into rifles, needing to be rammed down into the barrels. In 1848, French Captain Claude Minié invented a smaller bullet that expanded when fired, fitting smoothly into the grooves of the rifle.

FIRE IN THE HOLE
Firing from the Union rifled cannons caused breaches in Fort Pulaski's walls. Shells fired into the fort through these holes threatened to blow up the fort's artillery magazine, so the Confederates had to surrender.

THE BOMBARDMENT OF
FORT PULASKI

The Union also made use of the Parrott cannon during the Second Battle of Charleston Harbor.

MANY COASTAL FORTS PROTECTING SOUTHERN PORTS HAD THICK BRICK WALLS THAT OLDER CANNON FIRE COULD NOT PENETRATE.

In April 1862, Union Captain Quincy Gillmore prepared to attack Fort Pulaski. Its Confederate commander, Charles Olmstead, refused to surrender, but Gillmore had brought five 30-pounder Parrott cannons, whose rifled barrels allowed them to fire farther and more accurately. Stationed on nearby Tybee Island, Gillmore's artillery opened gaps in Pulaski's walls in two days, forcing Olmstead's surrender. Rifled cannons made traditional coastal defenses obsolete, further threatening the Confederacy's blockade-running activities.

FACT FILE

 LOCATION:
Fort Pulaski, near Savannah, Georgia

 DATE:
April 10–11, 1862

WHO WON:
Union

 CASUALTIES: Union 1; Confederacy 385

THE SHENANDOAH VALLEY
CAMPAIGN

IN MAY 1862, CONFEDERATE GENERAL THOMAS JACKSON WAS ORDERED TO TRY AND DIVERT UNION TROOPS THAT THREATENED RICHMOND.

In a 30-day campaign in the Shenandoah Valley, Jackson (see page 43) ran rings around his Union opponents, his troops undertaking 650 miles (1,050 km) of marches. Confederate victories in this valley, including those at Port Royal and Winchester, forced Lincoln to send reinforcements to the Valley, removing the immediate Union threat to Richmond.

FACT FILE

 LOCATION:
Shenandoah Valley, Virginia

 DATE:
March 23–June 9, 1862

 WHO WON:
Confederacy

 CASUALTIES: Union 4,865;
Confederacy 1,919

THE BATTLE OF CROSS KEYS
Confederate troops advance toward the front line at the Battle of Cross Keys in the valley's Rockingham County on June 8, 1862. They won a victory against feeble attacks by the Union.

LIFE ON THE
FRONT LINES

**MOST OF THE MEN WHO SIGNED UP FOR
THE ARMIES HAD NO EXPERIENCE OF WAR.**

After receiving basic training, most found themselves
in a very regimented life: in camp, they rose at 5 A.M.
and spent much of the day drilling, cleaning equipment,
or cooking. Music, playing cards, gambling, and reading
were some of the main forms of recreation.

Supplying such large armies was a challenge—rations
were mainly "hardtack" bread and salted pork, with
occasional vegetables. In the Confederate Army, rations
were lower, and new boots and uniforms were rarities.
On the march, troops got only an hour-long rest break,
and ill-fitting boots caused numerous foot injuries.
In crowded camps or trenches, disease was a serious
problem and twice as many Civil War soldiers died
of it as in battle.

> **❝ In the army, only captains
> and up had chairs. I hadn't sat
> in a chair in three years. ❞**
>
> Robert Strong, Union private in the 105th Illinois
> Infantry Regiment, on returning home

HARSH PUNISHMENT

Desertion was a
huge problem for
both armies, and
it was one of the
offenses (along with
pillaging and killing
civilians) for which
soldiers were regularly
sentenced to death.

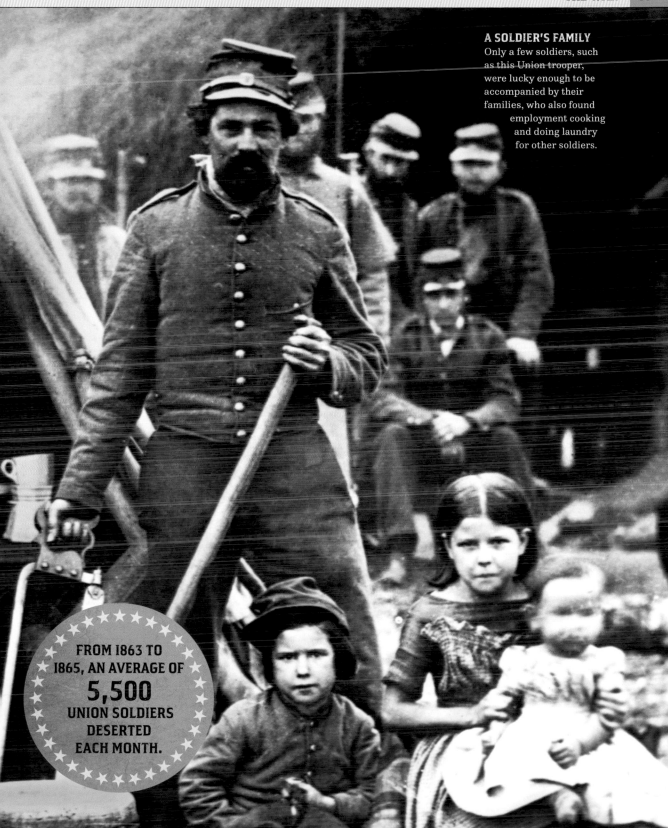

A SOLDIER'S FAMILY
Only a few soldiers, such
as this Union trooper,
were lucky enough to be
accompanied by their
families, who also found
employment cooking
and doing laundry
for other soldiers.

FROM 1863 TO
1865, AN AVERAGE OF
5,500
UNION SOLDIERS
DESERTED
EACH MONTH.

SUSIE KING
TAYLOR

SUSIE KING TAYLOR WAS BORN ON A PLANTATION IN GEORGIA IN 1848.

She escaped with her family to Union-occupied St. Simon's Island in 1862. There, she ran a school for African American adults and children before joining the 1st South Carolina Volunteer Regiment of the USCT (see pages 98–99) officially as a nurse, becoming the first African American military nurse.

She married a soldier in the regiment and accompanied him for the rest of the War. After the War, she wrote her book *Reminiscences of My Life in Camp*, a vivid account of her wartime experiences.

The front cover of Taylor's *Reminiscences of My Life in Camp*, published in 1902

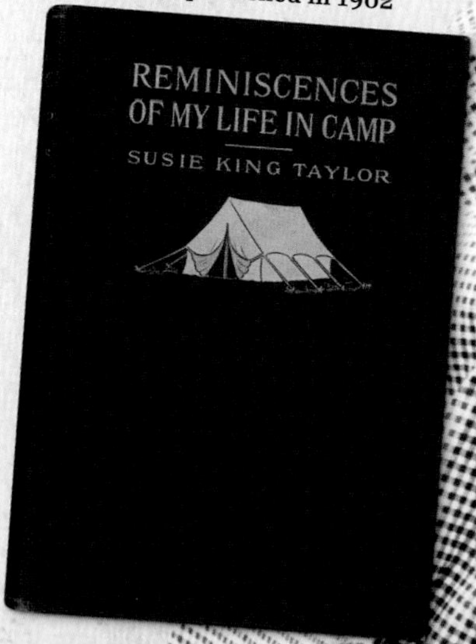

REMINISCENCES OF MY LIFE IN CAMP

SUSIE KING TAYLOR

FINAL YEARS
Susie King Taylor, seen here in a photograph taken in the 1880s, spent the rest of her life working with Woman's Relief Corps—an organization for female war veterans. She died 10 years after her book was published.

LOUISA MAY ALCOTT

ALCOTT CAME FROM A FAMILY OF ARDENT ABOLITIONISTS, WHO OPERATED A STATION ON THE UNDERGROUND RAILROAD.

In 1862, she volunteered as a nurse in the Union Army at Georgetown. A bout of typhoid forced her to leave after six weeks, but she published her experiences in a book called *Hospital Sketches* to help highlight the very unhygienic conditions she found there.

Most famous as the author of *Little Women*—which Alcott based on her early life—she later campaigned for girls' education.

The front cover of *Little Women*, which was first published as a novel in 1880

LITTLE WOMEN

Louisa May Alcott, photographed here at a writing desk, wrote *Little Women* when her publisher promised to publish her father's book if she wrote a novel with female characters.

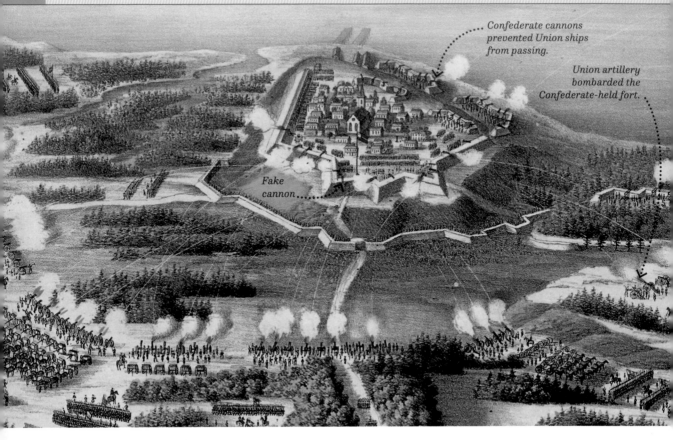

Confederate cannons prevented Union ships from passing.

Union artillery bombarded the Confederate-held fort.

Fake cannon

THE PENINSULA
CAMPAIGN
· ·

IN MARCH 1862, UNION GENERAL GEORGE B. McCLELLAN PLANNED TO ATTACK THE CONFEDERATE CAPITAL, RICHMOND.

McClellan (see page 78) transported a large army to the Virginia Peninsula, but then he hesitated, overestimating Confederate strength and allowing Confederate reinforcements to arrive under General Thomas "Stonewall" Jackson (see page 43).

When a reconnaissance around McClellan's lines revealed the Union line was weak on the right, Jackson attacked. In the Seven Days' Battle, beginning at Gaines' Mill on June 27, 1862, he sent McClellan retreating back down the peninsula.

CLEVER TACTICS

At the Siege of Yorktown (shown here)— a town near Chesapeake Bay—Confederate General John B. Magruder held up the Union Army for a month in April 1862. Magruder's maneuvers and construction of fake cannons (also known as "Quaker" guns) fooled McClellan into believing his force was far larger than it really was.

FACT FILE

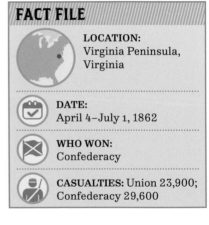

LOCATION:
Virginia Peninsula, Virginia

DATE:
April 4–July 1, 1862

WHO WON:
Confederacy

CASUALTIES: Union 23,900; Confederacy 29,600

BALLOON CORPS

AERIAL SURVEILLANCE
Portable inflation wagons helped fill the balloons with hydrogen on the battlefield. One of Lowe's balloons helped the Union at the Battle of Seven Pines in May 1862.

IN 1861, THE INVENTOR THADDEUS LOWE PERSUADED THE UNION ARMY TO USE BALLOONS FOR SPYING.

The balloons would be used by a branch of the Union Army called the Union Army Balloon Corps to monitor Confederate movements. Lowe built seven hydrogen balloons, which were tethered to ground stations.

The balloons were operated by civilian aeronauts, who signaled using flags or the telegraph (see page 104). They helped in several campaigns, notably the Peninsula Campaign in 1862. However, the vagueness of operators' intelligence reports and bad relations with military officers led to the dissolution of the Balloon Corps in 1863.

IT TOOK
3,600 FT (1,097 M)
OF SILK TO BUILD THE CANOPY OF ONE OF LOWE'S BALLOONS.

THE SECOND BATTLE OF
BULL RUN

ABOUT 119 MEN IN THE 5TH NEW YORK INFANTRY REGIMENT DIED IN LESS THAN 10 MINUTES OF ACTION.

IN AUGUST 1862, CONFEDERATE GENERAL ROBERT E. LEE DECIDED THAT BEFORE UNION TROOPS COULD REINFORCE GENERAL JOHN POPE IN VIRGINIA, HE MUST STRIKE FIRST.

He sent General Thomas Jackson (see page 43) with 24,000 men to march around the Union right flank and attack from behind. Pope moved to intercept but could not find Jackson until a Union division blundered into him near Manassas, Virginia. The next day, Pope sent uncoordinated attacks against the Confederate lines, which were all beaten back. By now, Confederate General James Longstreet had arrived to reinforce Jackson, but he held back. When Pope ordered an attack on the third day, Longstreet's divisions smashed into his advancing right flank, causing the Union soldiers to flee.

JAMES LONGSTREET

Shown here in uniform, James Longstreet was one of the Confederacy's leading generals. His initial holding back to attack at the Second Battle of Bull Run ended in a triumphant victory, but a repeat at Gettysburg in 1863 cast a shadow over his reputation.

RETREATING TROOPS

Union soldiers fell back after the second day of the Second Battle of Bull Run. Dejected and tired, they retreated to Washington, DC, raising fears that the Confederates might now attack the capital.

FACT FILE

LOCATION:
Bull Run/Manassas, Virginia

DATE:
August 28–30, 1862

WHO WON:
Confederacy

CASUALTIES: Union 13,824; Confederacy 8,353

EYEWITNESS: ELIZABETH HOBBS KECKLEY
FREE WOMAN

IN 1855, KECKLEY WAS ABLE TO PURCHASE HER FREEDOM AND OBTAIN A LEGAL DOCUMENT STATING THAT SHE WAS NO LONGER ENSLAVED.

"... in consideration of the sum of $1200, to me in hand paid this day in cash, hereby emancipate ... Lizzie, and her son George ...," read the deed of emancipation signed by Anne Garland, whose family had enslaved and mistreated Keckley for years.

Garland hired out Keckley as a seamstress, and her customers eventually loaned her the money with which she bought her freedom and that of her son. She would go on to be much in demand as a dressmaker for politicians' wives, including the First Lady, Mary Todd Lincoln.

Elizabeth Hobbs Keckley

CIVIL WAR MUSIC

THE VIBRANT POPULAR AND FOLK MUSIC OF THE MID-19TH CENTURY WAS TAKEN BY SOLDIERS ON CAMPAIGN.

Carrying portable instruments, such as banjos, fiddles, and bugles, they entertained themselves in camps, while fife-and-drum bands and trumpeters helped keep the beat during marches or signaled orders in battles. Musicians composed pieces as marching songs, such as *John Brown's Body*—popular with the Union troops—or songs to raise morale, such as *Dixie* in the South. Songs that expressed a desire for the end of the War, such as *When Johnny Comes Marching Home*, were also popular.

Bugle of Gustav Schurmann, a 12-year-old bugler with the Union's 40th New York Volunteer Infantry

When Johnny Comes Marching Home was composed by Irish American bandleader Patrick Gilmore.

British composer W. T. Wrighton's song, *Her bright smile haunts me still*, remembered a woman left behind at home.

Maple wood and ebony fife

The band of the Union's 10th Veteran Reserve Corps in Washington, DC

Violin of Private Solomon Conn of the Union Army

Eagle drum used by infantry on the march

Saxhorn with backward-facing bell, allowing it to be heard by troops behind the musician

ROBERT EDWARD LEE

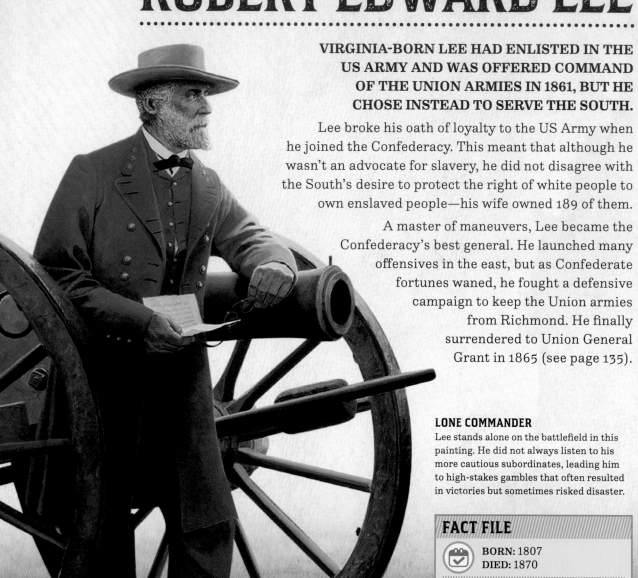

VIRGINIA-BORN LEE HAD ENLISTED IN THE US ARMY AND WAS OFFERED COMMAND OF THE UNION ARMIES IN 1861, BUT HE CHOSE INSTEAD TO SERVE THE SOUTH.

Lee broke his oath of loyalty to the US Army when he joined the Confederacy. This meant that although he wasn't an advocate for slavery, he did not disagree with the South's desire to protect the right of white people to own enslaved people—his wife owned 189 of them.

A master of maneuvers, Lee became the Confederacy's best general. He launched many offensives in the east, but as Confederate fortunes waned, he fought a defensive campaign to keep the Union armies from Richmond. He finally surrendered to Union General Grant in 1865 (see page 135).

LONE COMMANDER
Lee stands alone on the battlefield in this painting. He did not always listen to his more cautious subordinates, leading him to high-stakes gambles that often resulted in victories but sometimes risked disaster.

FACT FILE

 BORN: 1807
DIED: 1870

 RANK:
General-in-chief

 ARMY: Army of Northern Virginia, Confederacy

🎯 **1862:** Invades Maryland after victory at the Second Battle of Bull Run

1863: Suffers defeat at the Battle of Gettysburg

THE CONFEDERACY'S USE OF
SLAVE LABOR

ENSLAVED AFRICAN AMERICAN MEN DID NOT SERVE IN THE CONFEDERATE ARMY, BUT WERE FORCED TO TOIL AS LABORERS IN CAMPS AND ELSEWHERE.

As the Union Army approached the South, many enslaved people fled. The Union regarded them as "contraband of war," which meant they could be confiscated and then freed. Up to 700,000 slaves escaped during the War, seriously undermining the South's war effort. Only in March 1865 did the Confederacy pass a law allowing enslaved men to join the army, but it was never put into practice.

FORCED TO WORK

With such a high proportion of its male population in the army, the South's ability to fight the War depended heavily on slave labor. This woodcut engraving depicts enslaved African Americans drafted from plantations to work on fortifications in Savannah, Georgia.

Enslaved workers from plantations

Wagon used to transport excavated earth

CIVIL WAR LITERATURE

MANY AMERICAN AUTHORS WROTE A GREAT DEAL ABOUT THE CONFLICT.

Some authors, such as Harriet Beecher Stowe in *Uncle Tom's Cabin*, used their novels to argue against slavery. Others, including Walt Whitman and Herman Melville, served in the War and used their experiences to write about the suffering it caused. Louisa May Alcott employed the Civil War as a backdrop to *Little Women*, while others such as Mary Boykin Chesnut from South Carolina simply recorded what they saw.

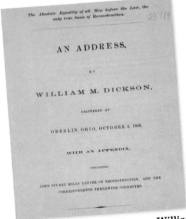

This 1865 work by Ohio lawyer William Dickson argues for the equality of former enslaved people before the law.

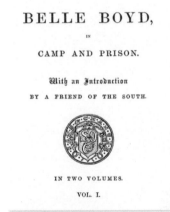

Confederate spy Belle Boyd's memoir *In Camp and Prison* talks about her experiences as a spy.

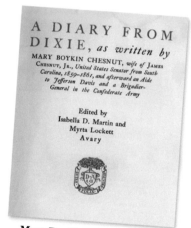

Mary Boykin Chesnut's diary, covering the years 1859–1861, illustrates her experiences during the War.

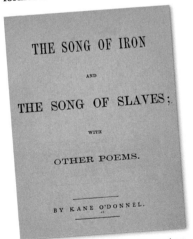

Journalist Kane O'Donnel's poetry collection is based on African American lyrics he collected in the South.

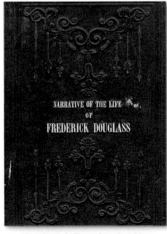

Frederick Douglass's 1845 autobiography is a powerful condemnation of slavery.

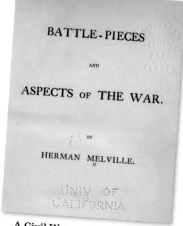

A Civil War poetry collection by Herman Melville, the author of the famous novel *Moby Dick*

THE MARYLAND CAMPAIGN

AFTER THE VICTORY AT THE SECOND BATTLE OF BULL RUN, CONFEDERATE GENERAL LEE DECIDED TO INVADE MARYLAND IN SEPTEMBER 1862.

He hoped to threaten Washington, DC, and lure Union General George McClellan (see page 78) into a decisive battle. Lee (see page 72) divided his forces into different columns, with one under General Thomas Jackson (see page 43) capturing the garrison at Harpers Ferry. Another, under Major General Daniel H. Hill, set up defensive lines at three gaps in South Mountain. Outnumbered in the Battle of South Mountain on September 14, Hill fell back, and Lee decided to regroup his entire army at Sharpsburg, Maryland, near the Potomac River and make a stand. Now he headed to Antietam (see pages 76–77).

FACT FILE

LOCATION: Maryland, Virginia

DATE: September 4–20, 1862

WHO WON: No victory for either side

CASUALTIES: Union 28,263; Confederacy 14,506

CROSSING THE POTOMAC

Lee's Army of Northern Virginia waded across the Potomac River, about 35 miles (56 km) from Washington, DC, at the start of the campaign. Many of the soldiers lacked boots, a sign of the Confederacy's supply problems.

HISTORICAL MAP

Seen here is part of a map of Antietam published in 1864 by the New York company H. H. Lloyd & Co. It was meant to show all of the battlefield graves in an effort to graphically depict the human toll of the War's bloodiest day.

Burnside Bridge ....

Antietam Creek ....

Graves on the battlefield ....

CROSSING THE CREEK

The 51st Pennsylvania Volunteers of the Union Army charged toward a bridge over Antietam Creek. Crossing it was essential in order to attack the Confederate Army's right flank, but the Union forces came under heavy fire each time they tried, crippling their advance. The bridge would later come to be known as the Burnside Bridge after Union General Ambrose Burnside.

THE BATTLE OF ANTIETAM

THE UNION SURRENDER AT HARPERS FERRY ENCOURAGED GENERAL LEE TO CONTINUE HIS MARYLAND CAMPAIGN.

However, Union General George B. McClellan's forces finally faced off with him at Antietam Creek near Sharpsburg. Lee had prepared his ground well, using groves of trees and a sunken road as formidable defensive positions. One part of the Union army, under General Joseph Hooker, attacked the Confederate left flank, and a bloody battle followed. However, McClellan's inability to coordinate attacks with his other troops left the Confederate center and right flanks relatively unchallenged. When their center was finally attacked, the Confederates took up positions in the sunken road. Vastly outnumbered, they fought off a series of attacks before retreating under heavy fire. The forces under Union General Ambrose Burnside tried to cross a bridge over Antietam Creek to get to the Confederate right flank but came under fire. Their delay in succeeding allowed Lee to resist, and he retreated the next day into Virginia. The Battle of Antietam, called the Battle of Sharpsburg by the Confederates, was the single bloodiest day of the War. Neither side won, but Lee's offensive had been stopped, making it a tactical victory for the Union.

FACT FILE

LOCATION:
Sharpsburg, Maryland

DATE:
September 17, 1862

WHO WON: No victory for either side

CASUALTIES: Union 12,401; Confederacy 10,316

GEORGE BRINTON
McCLELLAN

A MEXICAN-AMERICAN WAR VETERAN, McCLELLAN WAS CHOSEN TO HEAD THE ARMY OF THE POTOMAC AFTER ITS DEFEAT AT THE FIRST BATTLE OF BULL RUN.

Although an efficient organizer, he was overly cautious, and his bad relations with politicians were made worse by his slowness in moving his army forward. After the Peninsula Campaign (see page 66) in summer 1862, Lincoln dismissed McClellan, but he recalled him after the Second Battle of Bull Run (see pages 68–69). When he failed to pursue Lee after Antietam, the president removed him from command for good.

FACT FILE

 BORN: 1826
DIED: 1885

 RANK: General-in-chief

 ARMY: Army of the Potomac, Union

 1862: Steps down as general-in-chief to head Army of the Potomac

1862: During the Seven Days' Battles, Lee keeps McClellan from Richmond

CLIMBING THE LADDER
In this 1861 photograph, McClellan is pictured in a major general's uniform. He was promoted to this rank in 1861, before serving briefly as the Union Army's general-in-chief.

THE EMANCIPATION
PROCLAMATION

ABRAHAM LINCOLN DID NOT BEGIN THE WAR AIMING TO ABOLISH SLAVERY, BUT MANY REPUBLICANS ARGUED FOR THIS.

The Emancipation Proclamation issued by Lincoln in September 1862 declared that as of January 1, 1863, enslaved people in the rebelling Confederate states would be considered by the federal government to be free. This inspired many freed African Americans to volunteer for the Union Army. Now that freeing enslaved people was a clear war aim for the Union, it turned antislavery powers in Europe, such as Britain, away from aiding the Confederacy.

THE UNION'S PRESIDENT
Posters from the 1880s containing the text of Lincoln's Emancipation Proclamation associated the president with symbols of American freedom, such as the flag, the bald eagle, and the figures of Justice and Liberty.

The bald eagle is the national emblem of the USA.

Figure of Justice carrying the scales of justice and a sword

OVER
200,000
AFRICAN AMERICANS
JOINED THE UNION
FORCES BECAUSE OF
THE EMANCIPATION
PROCLAMATION.

Text of the Emancipation Proclamation

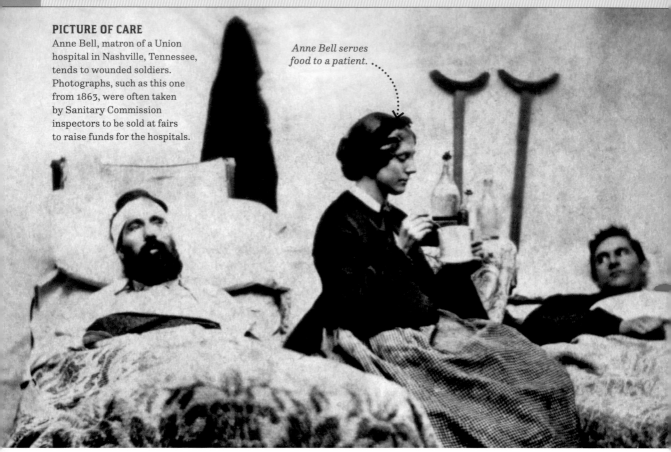

PICTURE OF CARE
Anne Bell, matron of a Union hospital in Nashville, Tennessee, tends to wounded soldiers. Photographs, such as this one from 1863, were often taken by Sanitary Commission inspectors to be sold at fairs to raise funds for the hospitals.

Anne Bell serves food to a patient.

THE WAR'S WOMEN

AS NURSES AND DOCTORS, WOMEN HELPED IN THE PROVISION OF MEDICAL CARE FOR THE WOUNDED.

Elizabeth Blackwell, the first woman in America to receive a medical degree, helped set up the United States Sanitary Commission in June 1861, whose volunteers instructed soldiers on hygiene. Dr. Mary E. Walker was at first denied a commission in the Union Army on account of her gender, but went on to serve as a surgeon with the Union's Army of the Cumberland. Pioneers such as the nurses Dorothea Dix and Clara Barton organized medical supplies for military hospitals, and Barton later founded the American Red Cross. Women also bore much of the burden of the War at home. Some worked as seamstresses, while others toiled on plantations and took care of their households.

Clara Barton raised funds for soldiers, worked as a nurse, and ran a program to locate missing soldiers.

FIGHTING IN
DISGUISE

ALTHOUGH WOMEN WERE NOT LEGALLY ALLOWED TO JOIN THE ARMY, SOME ENLISTED IN SECRET.

They disguised their gender in medical examinations and from their fellow soldiers in camp. A few hundred women actually fought, including Sarah Edmonds, who served in the Union's 2nd Michigan Infantry Regiment for two years as "Frank Thompson." Loreta Jane Vasquez, who fought for a Confederate Arkansas regiment, was wounded by a shell at Shiloh in 1862. Some even died—an anonymous woman was found among the Confederate dead after the Battle of Gettysburg.

> **❝ They fought like demons ... I saw three or four rebel women soldiers in the heap of bodies. ❞**
>
> Sergeant Robert Ardry, 111th Illinois Infantry Regiment, after a battle in Georgia in May 1864

SECRET SOLDIER
Frances Clalin Clayton enlisted alongside her husband in a Union Missouri regiment. Fighting as "Jack Williams," she was wounded three times and only finally revealed her identity after her husband was killed at the Battle of Stones River in January 1863.

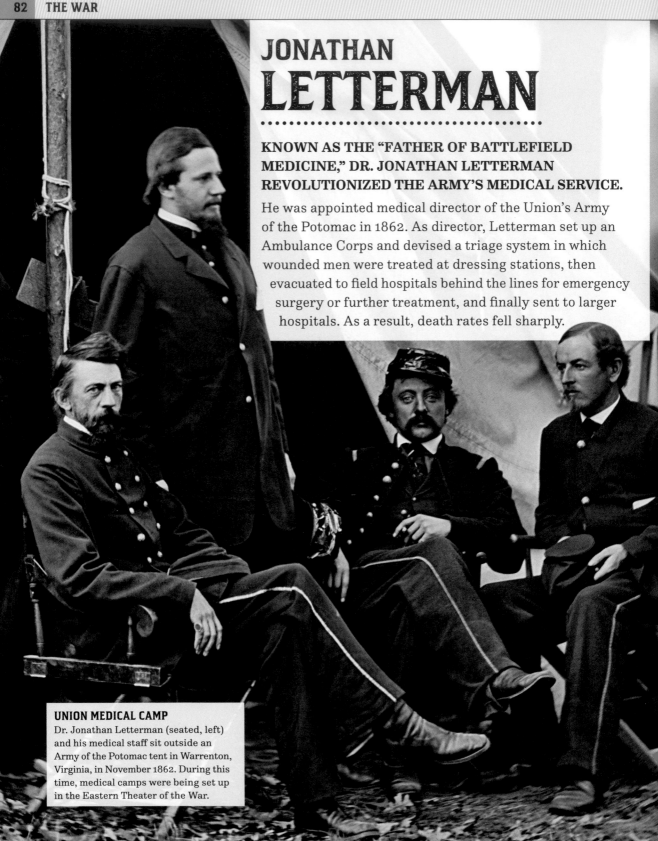

JONATHAN
LETTERMAN

KNOWN AS THE "FATHER OF BATTLEFIELD MEDICINE," DR. JONATHAN LETTERMAN REVOLUTIONIZED THE ARMY'S MEDICAL SERVICE.

He was appointed medical director of the Union's Army of the Potomac in 1862. As director, Letterman set up an Ambulance Corps and devised a triage system in which wounded men were treated at dressing stations, then evacuated to field hospitals behind the lines for emergency surgery or further treatment, and finally sent to larger hospitals. As a result, death rates fell sharply.

UNION MEDICAL CAMP

Dr. Jonathan Letterman (seated, left) and his medical staff sit outside an Army of the Potomac tent in Warrenton, Virginia, in November 1862. During this time, medical camps were being set up in the Eastern Theater of the War.

MEDICINE

AT THE START OF THE WAR, THE US ARMY HAD ONLY 30 SURGEONS, BUT BY JULY 1862 EACH UNION REGIMENT HAD A SURGEON.

Only then did conditions for wounded soldiers improve, with better-equipped divisional-level field hospitals and a Union Ambulance Corps, introduced in 1864. Many wounds needed amputations, but the lack of antiseptics and the rarity of anesthetics, coupled with unhygienic conditions, often led to fatal infections. Despite improvements in hygiene and organization, little could be done to combat disease.

Supply problems hampered Confederate attempts to maintain a similar system. Wounded soldiers were at first furloughed (sent home) or treated at large hospitals.

TREATING SOLDIERS

Union soldiers from a New York regiment tend to a wounded comrade in a Virginia field hospital in this 1861 photograph. There was little attempt to control hygiene in crowded tents like this one.

MEDICAL
EQUIPMENT

IN THE CIVIL WAR, DOCTORS HAD TO TREAT BOTH SOLDIERS SUFFERING FROM DISEASE AND THOSE WOUNDED IN COMBAT.

Because of this, the range of equipment they carried was wide but portable, with many able to fit in compact cases or rolls. Medicines for diseases were often ineffective, but medics carried them anyway. Most of their kit was for surgery and included sharp knives and saws to amputate injured limbs, which was the most common type of operation carried out following battles.

Wooden splint adjuster to keep broken leg immobile

Medicines used for pain relief

Crimper to remove bone fragments

Forceps to grasp bones during amputation

Clamps for use in surgery

Instructions with field tourniquet set, used to stop blood flow from a wound

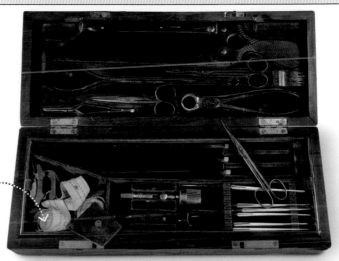

Large field amputation kit used by surgeons in the
13th Connecticut Volunteer Infantry Regiment

Portable medical bag could be used to carry items for immediate aid in the field.

Petit's tourniquet

Doctor's roll containing
medicines for easy access

ABOUT
60,000
AMPUTATION
SURGERIES WERE
CARRIED OUT
DURING THE
CIVIL WAR.

Trephine saw for removing
round bone sections

Saw with leaf-shaped blade
for skull incisions

Sharp amputation knife
for making clean cuts

Amputation knife
to cut soft tissue

Long-bladed
amputation knife

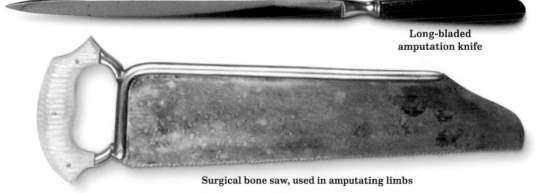

Surgical bone saw, used in amputating limbs

THE BATTLE OF
FREDERICKSBURG

IN NOVEMBER 1862, GENERAL AMBROSE BURNSIDE, WHO HAD REPLACED McCLELLAN AS THE UNION COMMANDER, DECIDED TO STRIKE AT RICHMOND.

He delayed crossing the wide Rappahannock River while pontoon bridges were built, but this allowed two Confederate forces under Generals Thomas Jackson (see page 43) and James Longstreet (see page 69) to unite to oppose him. Longstreet took position behind a stone wall on Marye's Heights, a low ridge overlooking the river, and when Union troops finally attacked, Confederate fire cut them down as they struggled to reach the wall. Burnside retreated the next morning, having suffered the worst Union defeat of the War.

FACT FILE

LOCATION:
Fredericksburg, Virginia

DATE:
December 11–15, 1862

WHO WON:
Confederacy

CASUALTIES: Union 12,653; Confederacy 5,377

FATEFUL CROSSING

Burnside's soldiers are seen building pontoon bridges so their army could cross the Rappahannock. He was delayed for a week due to the construction, allowing the Confederates to occupy strongpoints on the other side of the river.

EYEWITNESS: MARY BOYKIN CHESNUT
SOUTHERN ELITE

THE WIFE OF A SOUTH CAROLINA SENATOR, MARY BOYKIN CHESNUT RECORDED THE REACTION OF TRAIN PASSENGERS TO THE NEWS OF LINCOLN'S ELECTION AS PRESIDENT.

"The die is cast; no more vain regrets … the stake is life or death," she noted someone exclaiming. The moment marked a turning point for the South, the fortunes of which elite Chesnut chronicled in her diary.

Her account also recalled someone crying out, "Now that the Black radical Republicans have the power, I suppose they will Brown us all"—a reference to the mayhem caused by John Brown's raid at Harpers Ferry (see page 28). The secession of the Southern States brought an end to the way of life Chesnut and her social class had previously enjoyed.

Mary Boykin Chesnut

THE BATTLE OF
STONES RIVER

IN DECEMBER 1862, CONFEDERATE GENERAL BRAXTON BRAGG WAS PURSUED INTO TENNESSEE BY UNION GENERAL WILLIAM ROSECRANS.

Bragg's forces met Rosecrans's Army of the Cumberland at Stones River, where an initial attack by Bragg's men caught the Union soldiers at breakfast. Only a determined defense by Union General Philip Sheridan avoided defeat. After a pause, on January 2, Bragg ordered General John Breckinridge's Kentucky division into a near-suicidal charge. Hundreds died in a hail of Union artillery fire, and Bragg retreated farther into Tennessee, handing the Union Army and Lincoln a much-needed victory.

"ORPHANS" UNDER FIRE

Breckinridge's division was from Kentucky, which did not join the Confederacy, and his forces were considered the enemy by their home state. As a result, they were called the "Orphan Brigade." This painting shows the division charging across Stones River.

FACT FILE

LOCATION:
Murfreesboro, Kentucky

DATE: December 31, 1862– January 2, 1863

WHO WON: Union

CASUALTIES: Union 12,906; Confederacy 11,739

THE BATTLE OF
CHANCELLORSVILLE

IN LATE APRIL 1863, UNION COMMANDER JOSEPH HOOKER BEGAN A NEW CAMPAIGN IN VIRGINIA.

He divided his force in two and threatened Confederate General Lee's flank near the Wilderness. Lee (see page 72) reacted by dividing his own army in two. With one part, he attacked from the east on May 1, stopping Hooker's advance and forcing him back. The other part, under General Jackson (see page 43), marched along the back roads around the entire Union Army to launch a massive surprise attack from the west on May 2. After more heavy fighting on May 3, Hooker was forced to retreat in defeat. It was one of Lee's greatest triumphs, marred only by Jackson's accidental mortal wounding by his own troops.

FACT FILE

LOCATION:
Chancellorsville, Virginia

DATE:
April 30–May 6, 1863

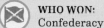

WHO WON:
Confederacy

CASUALTIES: Union 17,304; Confederacy 13,460

OUT OF THE WOODS

Having marched around the Union Army's flank, General Jackson leads his men out of thick woods to send the Union's 11th Corps into headlong retreat. Jackson would be fatally wounded later that day.

EYEWITNESS: J. E. B. STUART
CONFEDERATE COMMANDER

James Ewell Brown Stuart

IN A LETTER TO HIS COMMANDER, GENERAL J. E. B. STUART DISCUSSED HIS ATTACK STRATEGY.

Written to Brigadier General Fitzhugh Lee, Stuart's letter asked which of two Union forces he should attack during a campaign in Tennessee, saying, "I wish to concert with you some measures for attacking alternately, Kilpatrick and Gregg with my whole force …"

Stuart was impatient with more cautious officers and often distrustful of them. In his letter, he asked Lee, "Don't discuss the matter however with others."

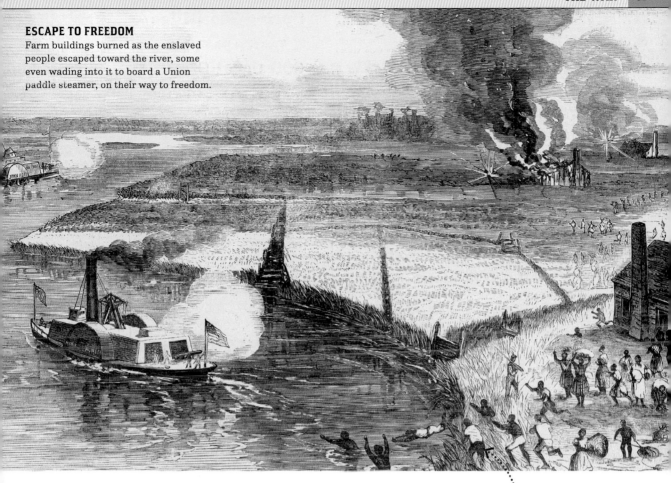

ESCAPE TO FREEDOM
Farm buildings burned as the enslaved
people escaped toward the river, some
even wading into it to board a Union
paddle steamer, on their way to freedom.

*Escapees await
the arrival of the
Union steamer.*

THE COMBAHEE
FERRY RAID

**DURING 1863, UNION FORCES BEGAN RAIDING
PLANTATIONS ALONG SOUTH CAROLINA'S COASTAL
RIVERS TO DISRUPT THE CONFEDERACY'S ECONOMY.**

On June 2, the 2nd South Carolina Infantry Regiment—a
unit of former enslaved African American people—sailed
up the Combahee River, hoping to free more people from
enslavement. Harriet Tubman (see page 25) became the
first American woman to lead a major military operation
when she led the Union regiment to plantations around
Combahee Ferry. Here, they fought off Confederate
defenders and freed around 800 enslaved people.

FACT FILE

LOCATION: Beaufort
and Colleton Counties,
South Carolina

DATE:
June 1–2, 1863

WHO WON:
Union

CASUALTIES: Union 0;
Confederacy 0

THE BATTLE OF
GETTYSBURG

HAVING CRUSHED THE UNION ARMY AT CHANCELLORSVILLE, GENERAL ROBERT E. LEE ONCE AGAIN INVADED THE NORTH, HOPING TO FORCE THE UNION INTO MAKING PEACE.

On July 1, 1863, Union General George Meade's Army of the Potomac caught up with Lee (see page 72) near Gettysburg in Pennsylvania and was nearly defeated by Lieutenant General Richard S. Ewell's Confederate division. The next day, Meade deployed the Union Army in a curved line similar to a fish hook from Culp's Hill in the north down to Little Round Top, which they successfully defended. On the third day, a desperate Lee ordered Major General Pickett to storm Cemetery Ridge in the Union center, but his men were cut down by a barrage of cannon and musket fire. Defeated, Lee retreated back to Virginia, ending the Confederacy's last realistic hope of winning the War.

OVER 7,000 SOLDIERS DIED, MAKING GETTYSBURG THE BLOODIEST OF ALL CIVIL WAR BATTLES.

PICKETT'S CHARGE

Waves of Confederate troops battle against the Union defenders of Cemetery Ridge during Pickett's Charge. More than 60 percent of the 12,500 Confederate attackers were killed, wounded, or captured.

FACT FILE

LOCATION:
Gettysburg,
Pennsylvania

DATE:
July 1–3, 1863

WHO WON:
Union

CASUALTIES: Union 23,049;
Confederacy 28,063

FIELD
ARTILLERY

ARTILLERY PLAYED A VITAL ROLE IN CIVIL WAR BATTLES, FIRING SHELLS THAT COULD DEVASTATE THE RANKS OF ADVANCING INFANTRY.

As these were heavy weapons, moving them needed a team of horses or a crew of many men. The bronze 12-pound "Napoleon" gun was the most common type early in the War. As the War went on, both sides introduced wrought-iron cannons with rifled barrels that could fire over a greater range and with more accuracy.

13-inch mortar nicknamed "The Dictator"

Grooves inside the iron barrel made the shot more stable.

Wooden base for attaching to cannon muzzle

Cannon trail with spike to move gun to left or right

12-pound solid shot for "Napoleon" gun, used for bombarding fortifications

20-pound Parrott gun with rifled barrel

Short barrel able to be raised to shoot at higher angles

Bronze "Napoleon" gun, a smoothbore cannon introduced in 1857

Pendulum Hausse Sight, used for sighting artillery shots

Howitzer trail with handle for moving from side to side

24-pound bronze howitzer, used at short range

CAMP LETTERMAN

DURING THE EARLY YEARS OF THE CIVIL WAR, MILITARY HOSPITALS WERE LOCATED IN TOWNS FAR BEHIND THE FRONT LINES.

The medical reforms of Union Medical Director Jonathan Letterman (see page 82) changed this. He created a Federal Ambulance Corps to evacuate the wounded off the field quickly. At Gettysburg, 4,000 Union soldiers were treated at a huge encampment of tents erected near the battlefield. This was known as "Camp Letterman," which finally closed in November 1863, four months after the battle.

MORE THAN 400 TENT WARDS WERE ERECTED AT CAMP LETTERMAN, EACH HOUSING 10 PATIENTS.

QUICK FIX

Army surgeons and volunteers from the US Sanitary Commission saved many lives by being able to operate quickly in the tents at Camp Letterman. This photograph shows an amputation scene at one of the surgeons' tents at the camp.

THE SIEGE OF
VICKSBURG

THE MISSISSIPPI RIVER WAS VITAL TO THE CONFEDERACY'S CONTROL OF ITS WESTERN REGIONS.

Dominating the river was Vicksburg, where swampy terrain west of the town made it difficult to maneuver. After a failed campaign to take the stronghold in late 1862, Union Admiral David D. Porter ran a flotilla of 12 boats past Vicksburg's guns on April 16, 1863.

Union Major General Ulysses S. Grant (see page 56) then moved on the town from the east, trapping Confederate garrison commander John C. Pemberton. By May 18, Vicksburg was under siege. A first assault on May 19 failed, but Union troops dug trenches and planted mines, preventing Confederate supplies from entering the town. Attempts by General Joseph E. Johnston to rescue Pemberton were unsuccessful. Finally, on July 3, Pemberton surrendered Vicksburg, its loss dealing a bitter blow to the Confederacy.

AFRICAN AMERICAN SOLDIERS

One of the first African American units in the Union Army successfully defended the garrison at Milliken's Bend near Vicksburg against a Confederate attack on June 7, 1863. The attack was intended to obstruct Union supplies and relieve Vicksburg.

UNDER FIRE

Confederate gun batteries that overlooked the Mississippi River made approaching Vicksburg by river daunting. Admiral Porter's gunboats had to run past them under heavy fire.

THE CONFEDERACY LOST VICKSBURG **THE DAY AFTER** ITS DEFEAT AT GETTYSBURG.

FACT FILE

LOCATION:
Vicksburg, Mississippi

DATE:
May 18–July 4, 1863

WHO WON:
Union

CASUALTIES: Union 4,910;
Confederacy 32,363

❝ Once let the Black man get ... a musket on his shoulder ... there is no power on Earth that can deny he has earned the right to citizenship. ❞

Frederick Douglass, April 6, 1863

UNITED STATES
COLORED TROOPS

AFRICAN AMERICAN MEN COULD NOT ENLIST UNTIL THE EMANCIPATION PROCLAMATION ALLOWED IT.

In January 1863, huge numbers of former enslaved African American men volunteered for the United States Colored Troops (USCT), which eventually grew to nearly 170 regiments and fought in many engagements. The most famous regiment was the 54th Massachusetts, which, in July 1864, led the Union attack on Fort Wagner, South Carolina. Despite this, the African American troops suffered discrimination, being paid less than white soldiers until late in 1864, and could not become officers.

They also risked enslavement or execution if captured by the Confederates. Their contribution to the Union cause was huge, with around 180,000 men serving in the USCT, of whom a fifth died in combat or of wounds or disease.

LINE OF DUTY
African American soldiers of the 4th US Colored Infantry Regiment are seen in this picture from 1865. The regiment's soldiers were awarded three Medals of Honor for gallantry at Chaffin's Farm, Virginia, in September 1864.

US COLORED TROOPS
FLAGS

AS WELL AS THE NATIONAL ARMY FLAG, EACH REGIMENT IN THE UNITED STATES COLORED TROOPS (USCT) HAD ITS OWN REGIMENTAL FLAG.

These acted as a rallying point for regimental pride for each of the more than 160 USCT regiments. Very few of the USCT flags have survived, but those that still exist bear images and slogans reflecting the African American soldiers' determination to help win freedom for the enslaved people of the South.

THE THIRD USCT'S FLAG CARRIED THE SLOGAN "RATHER DIE **FREEMEN** THAN LIVE TO BE SLAVES."

45th USCT flag with an African American soldier standing next to a bust of George Washington

Flag of the 26th New York Regiment, which fought in South Carolina in 1864–1865

Embroidered in the central stripe is "26 Regt. US Colored Troops."

Regulation national flag of the 26th New York Regiment with 35 stars, one for each state that existed at the time

Front of the 3rd USCT banner, showing an African American soldier holding a flag next to Columbia—a female symbol of the United States

84th USCT flag with a list of battles fought by the regiment

Back of the 3rd USCT banner

Soldier giving thanks for victory

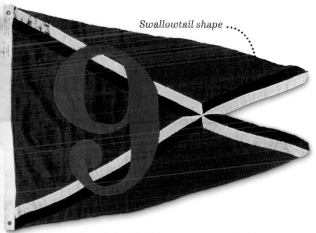

Swallowtail shape

Flag of the Chief Quartermaster of the 9th Army Corps, which included a USCT division

Flag of the 24th USCT Regiment designed by Philadelphia artist David Bustill Bowser

Notice of
Shaw's death
to his father

16

Beaufort S.Ca—

July 31st 1863

Col Shaw is killed. I regret to inform you that he was Col; The 54th Mass., of which Gilmore put them in a white Brigade. fought so bravely that Gen. When the attack was to be made on Fort Wagner. the Gen selected his best troops, and a the rest, the 54th. The black soldier side by side with their white in arms to the assault. (Tell to the world.) The parapet is Col. Shaw was the first man t high parapet. He waved d shouted come on boys', ll dead. He died will. nor home can excell

St. Helena I. July 4 1863

Dear Father,
All the troops excepting the colored Regiment are ordered to Folly Island — There will be a grand attack on Charleston. I suppose —
I feel very much disappointed at being left behind, especially after Montgomery & I were promised by Genl Gilmore that we should have our share in it.
I write you this lest you should see mention of this move —

EYEWITNESS: ROBERT GOULD SHAW
USCT COMMANDER

Robert Gould Shaw

SHAW WROTE OF HIS DISAPPOINTMENT AT HIS USCT REGIMENT BEING LEFT OUT OF AN IMPORTANT UNION ATTACK.

"There will be a grand attack on Charleston … I feel very much disappointed at being left behind …," he wrote to his father. Commander of the 54th Massachusetts Regiment of the US Colored Troops, Shaw fell four weeks later

while leading an attack on Fort Wagner. "When the attack was to be made … the Gen selected his best troops …," read his notice of death. The Confederate commander had Shaw's body buried with his men rather than returned. Intended as an insult, it instead highlighted Shaw's bravery and inspired many African Americans to enlist for the Union.

THE NEW YORK CITY
DRAFT RIOTS

VIOLENT PROTESTS
Armed rioters clash with the army on New York City's Fifth Avenue during the July 1863 anti-conscription riots. During four days of violence, at least 119 people were killed.

BOTH UNION AND CONFEDERATE GOVERNMENTS RESTRICTED CIVIL RIGHTS TO REDUCE OPPOSITION TO THEIR POLICIES AND CONDUCT OF THE WAR.

In 1861, Lincoln (see page 30) removed protections against being detained without trial, and Jefferson Davis (see page 29) followed in 1862. Free speech was curbed, and martial law was declared in the South.

Conscription (compulsory enlistment) into the army, and the ability of rich men to avoid it by paying for a substitute, was resented by the less fortunate. In 1863, there were riots against it in New York City, where the mob attacked African Americans, whom they blamed for the War.

THE UNION ARMY CALLED UPON **776,000** CONSCRIPTS TO SERVE, BUT ONLY 46,000 ACTUALLY DID SO.

THE TELEGRAPH

BOTH SIDES IN THE CIVIL WAR ADAPTED THE TELEGRAPH TO MILITARY PURPOSES, ALLOWING BATTLEFRONT NEWS TO PASS RAPIDLY TO RICHMOND AND WASHINGTON, DC.

The Union's Military Telegraph (USMT) Corps, formed in 1861, laid 15,000 miles (24,140 km) of lines during the War. Field telegraphs gave news of the defeat at Chickamauga in September 1863, allowing the Union to assemble dozens of trains to send 20,000 reinforcements to Chattanooga (see page 108). Both sides encoded their telegraph messages, but the Union cracked the Confederate cipher, giving them a huge intelligence advantage.

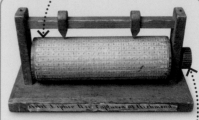

Alphabet and symbols for encoding messages

Confederate cipher wheel used to encode messages

Lever to move the circular drum

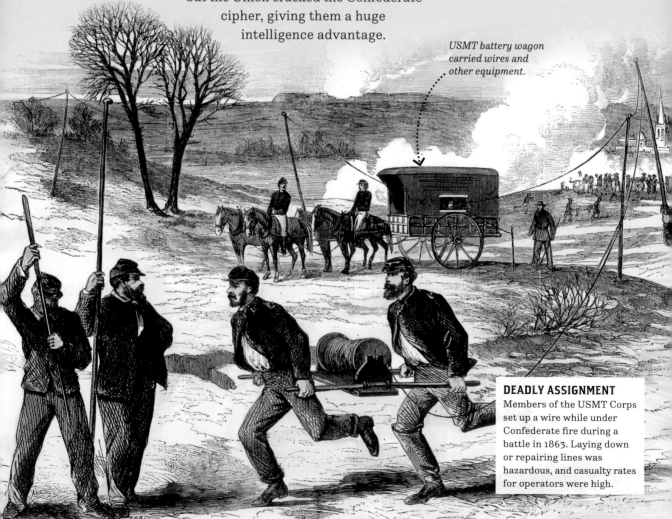

USMT battery wagon carried wires and other equipment.

DEADLY ASSIGNMENT
Members of the USMT Corps set up a wire while under Confederate fire during a battle in 1863. Laying down or repairing lines was hazardous, and casualty rates for operators were high.

THE BATTLE OF
CHICKAMAUGA

GOING HEAD-TO-HEAD
Union and Confederate troops fire at close quarters at the height of the battle, as seen in this color print. For his stubborn defense, Union General George Henry Thomas earned the nickname "The Rock of Chickamauga."

IN EARLY SEPTEMBER 1863, AN ADVANCE BY UNION GENERAL WILLIAM ROSECRANS INTO GEORGIA THREATENED TO SPLIT THE CONFEDERACY IN TWO.

Confederate President Jefferson Davis (see page 29) sent General Braxton Bragg to head him off, and the two forces met at Chickamauga. On the first day, Bragg's attack failed to outflank Rosecrans, but late the next morning, reinforcements under Lieutenant General James Longstreet (see page 69) surged through a gap that had opened up in the Union center. Large parts of Rosecrans's army fled, but Bragg's failure to follow up allowed Rosecrans to escape to Chattanooga (see page 108), where he soon found himself under Confederate siege.

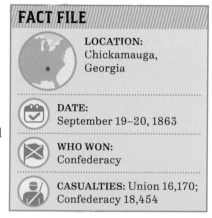

FACT FILE

LOCATION:
Chickamauga, Georgia

DATE:
September 19–20, 1863

WHO WON:
Confederacy

CASUALTIES: Union 16,170; Confederacy 18,454

CIVIL WAR
NEWS

DURING THE CIVIL WAR, BEFORE BROADCAST MEDIA, MOST PEOPLE RECEIVED THE NEWS IN NEWSPAPERS.

These often presented an optimistic view of their side's progress as a means of raising morale. Many popular newspapers were illustrated, using cartoons to criticize politicians and policies they disliked. Journalists accompanied the armies and were able to use the new technology of the telegraph (see page 104) to transmit reports for publication within hours of a battle.

The *New York Herald's* account of Antietam includes a map to help readers understand the battle.

Harper's Weekly brings a vivid depiction of the bombardment of Fort Sumter to its readers.

The *Washington Evening Star* reports the terms of General Lee's surrender at Appomattox in April 1865.

The *Staunton Spectator* reports the 1863 victory at Chancellorsville from a Confederate perspective.

The *New York Times* report on Lincoln's assassination sums it up in two words: "Awful Event."

GEORGE HENRY
THOMAS

DEFYING EXPECTATIONS THAT HE WOULD JOIN THE SOUTH, SOUTHERNER GEORGE HENRY THOMAS BECAME ONE OF THE UNION'S TOP GENERALS.

A veteran of the Mexican-American War, Thomas was a patient and logical leader rather than a flamboyant commander. He was second-in-command at Stones River, became the Union's "Rock of Chickamauga," and led the Army of the Cumberland to victory at Missionary Ridge (see page 108). His victory against Confederate General John Bell Hood at Nashville (see page 127) in December 1864 destroyed one of the last large Confederate armies. After the War ended, Thomas stayed on as military governor of Tennessee.

FACT FILE

 BORN: 1810
DIED: 1870

RANK:
Major General

 ARMY: Army of the
Cumberland, Union

 1863: Breaks Confederate
siege of Chattanooga

1863: Wins against Braxton
Bragg at Missionary Ridge

1864: Defeats John Bell
Hood's army at Nashville

LOYAL FOLLOWER
In this photograph from 1865, Thomas wears the uniform of a major general. A loyal subordinate, he served as Sherman's second-in-command during the Atlanta Campaign before winning his own victory at Nashville.

THE CHATTANOOGA
CAMPAIGN

CONFEDERATE GENERAL BRAGG'S PLAN TO STARVE OUT A DEMORALIZED WILLIAM ROSECRANS TRAPPED IN CHATTANOOGA WAS FOILED BY GRANT.

Appointed to replace Rosecrans, on November 24, 1863, Grant sent Union commanders Joseph Hooker and William T. Sherman (see page 129) to take Lookout Mountain, one of the heights above Chattanooga, but the Confederates remained entrenched on nearby Missionary Ridge. The next day, General George H. Thomas ordered four Union divisions up to the ridge, where to everyone's astonishment, they charged to the top and broke the siege. Bragg retreated, and the way now lay open to Atlanta.

FACT FILE

LOCATION:
Chattanooga, Tennessee

DATE:
November 23–25, 1863

WHO WON:
Union

CASUALTIES: Union 5,824; Confederacy 6,667

SURPRISE ATTACK

Union soldiers attack up the steep slopes of Missionary Ridge in this engraving. The Confederates were so surprised that the Union attackers reached them before they could fire more than two shots.

DARING DEFENSE
Many Irish Americans also joined the Confederate Army. Their highest-ranking officer was Brigadier General Patrick R. Cleburne, seen here leading a determined defense against Union attacks at Chickamauga in 1863.

Patrick R. Cleburne

IMMIGRANT
OUTFITS

LARGE NUMBERS OF EUROPEAN IMMIGRANTS FROM THE NORTH ENLISTED IN THE UNION ARMY, WHILE SOME JOINED THE CONFEDERATE FORCES.

In the Union Army, some immigrants served in mixed regiments, while others were part of outfits made up mainly of immigrants, such as the Irish Brigade. About 200,000 Germans enlisted, as did many Italians with military experience in Europe.

Unfair allegations of looting made many immigrant outfits unpopular, although some produced high-ranking officers, such as General Franz Sigel, who helped the Union win at Pea Ridge in 1862.

Recruitment poster for German immigrants

PHOTOGRAPHY

The Civil War was the first conflict to be extensively captured from beginning to end by photography. Photographers such as Mathew Brady, Alexander Gardner, and George Smith Cook were some of the first to document the War. Photographic equipment was cumbersome, needing long exposures, glass plates, and complex processes to coat chemicals onto wet plates to develop the image, so photographers traveled in wagons that doubled as dark-rooms. Action shots were nearly impossible and most photographs were portraits, often taken as mementos before the men went to war. Some of the most striking shots are of fallen soldiers on the battlefield.

Wooden frame for holding lens

Movable section allowed camera to change focus

Stereoscope used to view three-dimensional (3-D) images by blending two separate photographs

John Carbutt, who photographed Union soldiers in Kentucky, poses with his camera.

Globe wide-angle lens

Camera with C. C. Harrison Globe lens—the first practical wide-angle lens—and bottles for chemicals used in developing the image

An African American Union soldier
poses with his family.

Mathew Brady (second from right) and other
photographers in a camp at Berlin, Maryland

Union soldiers sheltering in a trench before the
Second Battle of Fredericksburg, 1863, as
photographed by Captain Andrew J. Russell

Photographic wagon and camera of Sam Cooley,
who documented the War around Beaufort,
South Carolina, and elsewhere

A "powder monkey," a young boy who carried powder to the gun
crews, stands by a gun on the Union ship USS New Hampshire.

A photographer uses a tripod to photograph
a bridge near Knoxville, Tennessee.

A NATIONAL HOLIDAY:
THANKSGIVING

Sarah Josepha Hale

THERE WAS NO NATIONAL DAY OF CELEBRATION FOR THANKSGIVING BEFORE THE CIVIL WAR.

Although President George Washington had called for a day of Thanksgiving, individual states held Thanksgivings at different times.

American writer Sarah Josepha Hale, who penned the children's poem *Mary Had a Little Lamb*, spent nearly three decades lobbying the government to make Thanksgiving a national holiday.

On October 3, 1863, in gratitude for the victory at Gettysburg (see pages 92–93), President Lincoln (see page 30) issued a proclamation making the last Thursday in November "a day of Thanksgiving and Praise," which he hoped would "help heal the wounds of the nation." Since then, it has become the United States' best-known holiday.

CELEBRATING THANKSGIVING
The reaction of various groups to the declaration of Thanksgiving is shown in this 1863 illustration. It includes the figure of liberty—prominently present at the center—and the emancipated enslaved people in the central panel at the bottom.

LINCOLN'S
GETTYSBURG ADDRESS

ON NOVEMBER 19, 1863, PRESIDENT ABRAHAM LINCOLN GAVE AN ADDRESS THAT BECAME ONE OF THE MOST FAMOUS SPEECHES IN AMERICAN HISTORY.

He spoke at the dedication of a new cemetery for the soldiers who had fallen in the Battle of Gettysburg. Speaking after Edward Everett, a former Massachusetts governor, Lincoln delivered fewer than 275 words, warning that it still remained for the country to ensure "that government of the people, by the people, for the people, shall not perish from the earth."

LARGER THAN LIFE
Dressed in his characteristic black suit and speaking from a platform, Lincoln—at more than 6 ft (1.8 m) tall—towered over the thousands in the crowd as he delivered the Gettysburg Address.

EVERETT'S SPEECH LASTED FOR NEARLY 2 HOURS, WHILE LINCOLN SPOKE FOR **3 MINUTES.**

TRIUMPH AT TEXAS

A Union gunship is ablaze off Galveston, Texas, during a Confederate attack in January 1863. Brigadier General John Magruder retook the city, allowing the South to retain one major port until the War's end. This was an important victory in the Western Theater (area in the West where conflicts took place).

Union gunboat on fire

THE WESTERN
THEATER

WEST OF THE MISSISSIPPI, THE UNION FORCES AIMED TO SEIZE TEXAS AND THE CONFEDERACY HAD ITS EYE ON CALIFORNIA.

A Union invasion failed at Sabine Pass in September 1863, and they did not take the key town of Galveston until 1865. In the far west, Confederate Brigadier General Henry Sibley's forces marched from Arizona to California but were halted at Glorieta Pass in New Mexico Territory in March 1862. Many of his soldiers died of hunger or thirst during the retreat. The War in

Confederate guerrilla William Quantrill's raiders attacked and killed more than 150 men and boys in Lawrence, Kansas, on August 23, 1863.

the far west then devolved into skirmishes and raids, many against American Indian groups who had little involvement in the War.

CIVIL WAR
CURRENCY

TO HELP PAY FOR THE WAR, THE UNION GOVERNMENT ISSUED THE FIRST FEDERAL PAPER CURRENCY IN 1862.

These Union "greenbacks"—nicknamed for their color—generally held their value. The Confederate Congress also issued banknotes, as did individual Southern states, but these were of poor quality and easily forged. Their worth was distrusted by the people as the blockaded South suffered deprivation and defeats. This caused the value of these banknotes to fall. A Confederate dollar at the end of 1863 was only worth one-seventh of its original value.

The 1864 Confederate $5 bill issued by the State of Alabama showed an overseer supervising enslaved field workers.

The 1861 "demand note" for $5 issued by the Union could be used to pay for taxes and customs dues but not other goods.

This is an extremely rare 1861 Confederate 1-cent coin. Only around 20 were ever minted.

Head of Liberty surrounded by 13 stars ....

The 1864 "Liberty Head" $20 gold coin was nicknamed the "double eagle." It was the highest-value coin in circulation in the Union.

The $50 bill, issued in Richmond in 1861, bore the head of Confederate President Jefferson Davis.

This 1862 $50 bill bearing George Washington's portrait was one of the first Union banknotes in general circulation.

EYEWITNESS: JOHN ROSS
CHEROKEE CHIEF

John Ross

Lincoln's response to Ross's letter

ROSS WROTE TO PRESIDENT LINCOLN EXPLAINING WHY MANY OF HIS PEOPLE HAD ALLIED WITH THE CONFEDERACY.

"That no other alternative was left them, surrounded by the Power …," he wrote. In his letter, he said that the Cherokee, surrounded by the Confederates, had been forced to cooperate with them but had since shown their loyalty to the Union. Lincoln's response was cautious and even-handed, making no promises toward the Cherokee. "Neither have I been able to investigate … the exact … facts claimed by you …," he replied. Ross had initially called for his people to remain neutral during the War, but the Cherokee were divided on the issue.

FIGHTERS IN RECOVERY
Wounded American Indian troops are treated after the Battle of the Wilderness. They are probably from the 1st Michigan Sharpshooters Company K, a unit that included many Chippewa and Ottawa American Indians.

STAND WATIE WAS THE **LAST** CONFEDERATE GENERAL TO SURRENDER IN THE WAR.

AMERICAN INDIANS
IN THE WAR

Brigadier General Stand Watie, Cherokee chief, was the Confederacy's most senior American Indian officer.

BOTH SIDES TRIED TO RECRUIT AMERICAN INDIANS AS ALLIES.

The Confederates gained the support of some people from the Cherokee, Creek, Chickasaw, Choctaw, and Seminole tribes—many of whose warriors acted as scouts and raiders. Other tribes, including the Delaware, Seneca, and Iroquois, fought for the Union in many battles, including the Wilderness (see page 119). American Indian lands suffered widespread destruction of livestock, the burning of villages—often of tribes with little or no connection to the warring sides—and food shortages. After the War, those such as the Cherokee, who had largely sided with the Confederacy, were punished by having their previous Treaties with the US government canceled and harsh new terms imposed.

ANDERSONVILLE
PRISON

AROUND 400,000 SOLDIERS WERE TAKEN PRISONER DURING THE CIVIL WAR.

Some never made it to prison camps. At Fort Pillow, in April 1864, Confederate troops massacred dozens of surrendering African American soldiers.

In the early years, soldiers were often paroled or released in prisoner exchanges, but this stopped in 1863. Prisoners were now sent to ill-equipped camps, many of which were exposed to the weather and became breeding grounds for disease. The worst was the overcrowded Confederate camp of Andersonville in Georgia, which held more than 45,000 Union prisoners in appalling conditions. Almost 13,000 of them died.

Confederate forces shoot African American soldiers at Fort Pillow.

CAMP QUARTERS

The stockade around the Andersonville prison camp is pictured in this Civil War-era photograph, with the prisoners' tents in the foreground. Conditions were so bad at this prison that, after the War, its Confederate commander Henry Wirz was tried for war crimes and executed.

Stockade

Rows of prisoners' tents

FIGHTING BLIND
Union troops advance through the Wilderness to attack the Confederates. The thick woods caused both sides problems: smoke among the trees made it hard to see the enemy, and sparks from guns caused fires in the undergrowth.

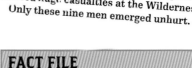

The Union's 57th Massachusetts Regiment suffered huge casualties at the Wilderness. Only these nine men emerged unhurt.

THE BATTLE OF THE
WILDERNESS

IN MAY 1864, GRANT ADVANCED ACROSS THE RAPIDAN RIVER, HOPING TO CROSS THE DENSELY WOODED MARSHY LAND CALLED THE WILDERNESS.

His plan of outflanking the Confederate Army of Northern Virginia failed when Lee (see page 72) reacted quickly, slamming into Grant (see page 56) with just one-third of his force. But Grant recovered, and the next day, bitter fighting erupted again. Although Lieutenant General James Longstreet (see page 69) arrived with Confederate reinforcements, it was not enough, and both sides dug entrenchments. Finally, Grant slipped away to try to outflank Lee again by heading for the junction at Spotsylvania (see page 120).

FACT FILE

 LOCATION: Spotsylvania and Orange County, Virginia

 DATE: May 5–7, 1864

 WHO WON: No victory for either side

 CASUALTIES: Union 17,000; Confederacy 13,000

THE BATTLE OF
SPOTSYLVANIA COURTHOUSE

FACT FILE

LOCATION:
Spotsylvania
Courthouse, Virginia

DATE:
May 8–21, 1864

WHO WON: No victory
for either side

CASUALTIES: Union 18,000;
Confederacy 12,000

THE OVERLAND CAMPAIGN BEGAN IN 1864, WHEN UNION GENERAL GRANT CROSSED THE RAPIDAN RIVER TO ADVANCE YET AGAIN ON RICHMOND.

After the Battle of the Wilderness (see page 119), Grant raced toward Spotsylvania Courthouse to place himself between Confederate General Lee and Richmond, but a part of Lee's army under Major General Richard H. Anderson arrived first and built a formidable set of entrenchments. For 12 days, Grant hurled his men against these, with rain turning the trenches into mud-choked death traps. Thousands died in the battle. Finally, Grant disengaged and again tried to maneuver around Lee's army.

STORMING FORWARD

Drenched in torrential rain, Union soldiers advance toward a Confederate-held earthwork, typical of the defenses whose capture cost Grant's army thousands of casualties at Spotsylvania Courthouse.

Defender carrying Confederate flag

Union soldiers advance with their flag.

Springfield rifled musket

THE BATTLE OF
COLD HARBOR

IN LATE MAY 1864, GENERAL GRANT HEADED TOWARD COLD HARBOR, TRYING TO PLACE HIMSELF BETWEEN GENERAL LEE AND RICHMOND.

Again, Confederate General Lee got there first. An initial Union assault nearly broke through, but the Confederates held and used a pause in fighting to construct strong entrenchments. Grant sent a head-on assault into these on June 3. Many Union attackers fell before they could reach the zigzag of the Confederate defenses. It was Grant's worst defeat, and now he changed tactics, making for the strategic rail hub of Petersburg (see page 124).

COSTLY ASSAULT
The Union Army's 18th Corps charges Confederate rifle pits at the height of Cold Harbor, an attack that cost them more than 2,500 casualties and ended up being repelled by the Confederates.

FACT FILE

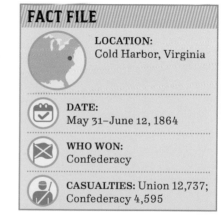

LOCATION:
Cold Harbor, Virginia

DATE:
May 31–June 12, 1864

WHO WON:
Confederacy

CASUALTIES: Union 12,737; Confederacy 4,595

CONFEDERATE SPIES, RAIDERS, AND SCOUTS

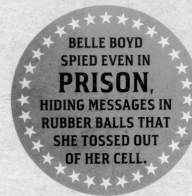

BELLE BOYD SPIED EVEN IN **PRISON,** HIDING MESSAGES IN RUBBER BALLS THAT SHE TOSSED OUT OF HER CELL.

The Confederates operated several spy rings in Washington, DC, to gain information about Union political and military plans. As Union armies advanced into the South, civilians also began to pass military information to the Confederacy.

ROSE O'NEAL GREENHOW
Greenhow used her friendship with senior Washington politicians to pass information to the Confederacy.

JOHN SINGLETON MOSBY
Mosby led a band of raiders and scouts that created havoc behind Union lines in Virginia.

JOHN YATES BEALL
A privateer, Beall was hanged for trying to free Confederate prisoners-of-war around Sandusky Bay, Ohio.

ANTONIA FORD
Ford was arrested for her role in Mosby's kidnapping of Union General Edwin Stoughton.

BENJAMIN FRANKLIN STRINGFELLOW
Stringfellow was Confederate General J. E. B. Stuart's personal scout. He was so effective that the Union offered a $10,000 reward for his capture.

BELLE BOYD
Known as the "Belle Rebelle," Boyd made friends with Union officers to extract their secrets.

UNION SPIES, DETECTIVES, AND SCOUTS

AFRICAN AMERICAN SPIES **BEHIND** CONFEDERATE LINES PROVIDED INTELLIGENCE TO THE UNION.

The Union relied on civilian spies, some in Richmond, and had a military information bureau run by detectives. The Union Army employed spies in uniform called scouts. Many African American escapees from the South and former enslaved people helped the Union as well.

ELIZABETH VAN LEW
A Richmond resident, Van Lew sent regular messages to Union officials and hid escaped Union prisoners in her mansion.

ALLAN PINKERTON
Detective agency head Pinkerton often overestimated Confederate troop numbers, which made General McClellan too cautious in the Peninsula Campaign.

LAFAYETTE C. BAKER
Baker cracked down on Southern supporters in the North and led the pursuit of assassin John Wilkes Booth after he killed Abraham Lincoln.

GEORGE H. SHARPE
Head of the Union Bureau of Military Information from 1863 to 1865, Sharpe insisted on the proper analysis of intelligence collected by spies.

WILLIAM A. JACKSON
Jefferson Davis's coachman, Jackson escaped to the North and gave the Union vital information about the Confederate president.

PAULINE CUSHMAN
An actress, Cushman accompanied the Confederate Army through Kentucky and Tennessee, all the while sending their secrets to Union agents.

THE SIEGE OF
PETERSBURG

AFTER COLD HARBOR, ULYSSES S. GRANT MADE FOR PETERSBURG BUT WAS DENIED AN EASY VICTORY.

Confederate Brigadier General P. G. T. Beauregard's 2,500 defenders held off the initial Union attack. After reinforcements, the two sides built hundreds of miles of trenches and settled down into a grueling 10-month siege. On July 30, 1864, Union engineers caused a massive explosion, creating a crater through which the 23rd United States Colored Troops (USCT) Regiment surged, but failed to break the Confederate line, 272 of the 400 men in the unit falling to enemy fire. At huge cost, Grant ground Lee down, cutting road and rail links. Finally, on April 2, 1865, he took Petersburg with a massive assault.

FACT FILE

LOCATION:
Petersburg, Virginia

DATE:
June 15, 1864–April 2, 1865

WHO WON:
Union

CASUALTIES: Union 42,000; Confederacy 28,000

LINE OF SUPPLY

A Union convoy carrying provisions passes through Petersburg after its capture by Union forces. Grant's ability to supply his army and to choke off Confederate supply lines played a key role in the city's fall.

Wagon train carrying provisions

President Lincoln in a stovepipe hat

PRESIDENTIAL TARGET

President Lincoln stands on the walls of Fort Stevens. The fighting was less than 3 miles (5 km) north of Lincoln's summer residence at Soldier's Home and the president was eager to see it, but he had to be ordered off the parapet to avoid being shot.

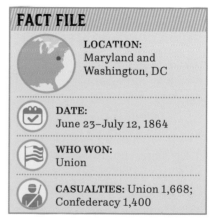

Jubal Anderson Early pictured as a lieutenant general

EARLY'S INCURSION INTO
MARYLAND

IN JULY 1864, CONFEDERATE LIEUTENANT GENERAL JUBAL EARLY STRUCK INTO MARYLAND TO TRY TO PULL UNION FORCES AWAY FROM RICHMOND.

He aimed to do this by threatening Washington, DC. Early found his way almost unopposed and reached within 5 miles (8 km) of the White House before coming up against Fort Stevens. He wasted a day in probing its defenses, allowing Union reinforcements to reach it. After some brief skirmishes, he decided not to attack and retreated to Virginia. It was the closest the Confederate Army ever got to the US capital.

FACT FILE

LOCATION:
Maryland and Washington, DC

DATE:
June 23–July 12, 1864

WHO WON:
Union

CASUALTIES: Union 1,668; Confederacy 1,400

Farragut on the ship's rigging

Sailors reload cannon.

THE BATTLE OF
MOBILE BAY

AS WAR RAGED ON LAND BETWEEN THE UNION AND THE CONFEDERACY, BOTH SIDES TUSSLED AT SEA.

In February 1864, the CSS *Hunley* became the first submarine to sink a ship when its torpedo (contact mine) struck the Union warship USS *Housatonic* in Charleston Harbor. On August 5, Union Admiral David Farragut (see page 57) attacked Fort Morgan in Mobile Bay, aiming to destroy the Confederate fleet in Alabama and take one of its last open ports. He ordered his fleet to sail straight through a minefield and overcame a single-handed resistance by the Confederacy's ironclad CSS *Tennessee* to force the fort's surrender.

MINEFIELD CROSSING
Admiral Farragut stands aboard his flagship USS *Hartford* as it sails toward Fort Morgan. When warned of the minefield, he is quoted to have said "Damn the torpedoes," before going full speed ahead.

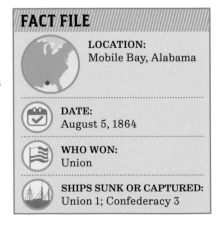

FACT FILE

LOCATION:
Mobile Bay, Alabama

DATE:
August 5, 1864

WHO WON:
Union

SHIPS SUNK OR CAPTURED:
Union 1; Confederacy 3

TAKING FRANKLIN AND
NASHVILLE

IN NOVEMBER 1864, CONFEDERATE GENERAL JOHN BELL HOOD STILL THOUGHT HE COULD REVERSE THE WAR'S COURSE AND ADVANCE INTO KENTUCKY.

He chased Union General John Schofield to Franklin, where on November 30, he sent 22,000 southerners into the War's last great charge. Thousands fell, but he dislodged Schofield, who retreated north to Nashville. There, over two days, Major General George H. Thomas and Schofield combined diversionary attacks on Hood's right with smashing blows to his left until the Confederates broke and fled. The USCT played a key role in the Union effort.

The Army of the Tennessee was no more.

FACT FILE

 LOCATIONS:
Franklin and
Nashville, Tennessee

 DATES:
November 30, 1864
(Franklin), December
15–16, 1864 (Nashville)

WHO WON:
Union

 CASUALTIES: Union 5,387;
Confederacy 12,200

FATAL ATTACK
Confederate General Patrick R. Cleburne (on horseback) led his men in a desperate assault at Franklin to clear the Union troops out of their entrenchments. Moments later, he and hundreds of his men were dead.

THE ATLANTA AND SAVANNAH
CAMPAIGNS

IN MAY 1864, GENERAL WILLIAM TECUMSEH SHERMAN BEGAN AN ADVANCE INTO GEORGIA.

He dueled with Confederate General Joseph E. Johnston, who held him up at strong defensive positions, only for Sherman to outflank them each time. By mid-July he had reached Atlanta, which Confederate General John Bell Hood, now in command, defended aggressively but had to evacuate on September 1, when the Union Army circled around and cut a key rail route.

Sherman engaged in a destructive "March to the Sea," with his troops looting and burning a 60-mile (96-km) wide area all the way to Savannah, which they took on December 22. The Confederacy was now cut in two.

BREAKING THE LINES
The Union Army tore up around 200 miles (320 km) of railroad track during the "March to the Sea," seriously disrupting the Confederacy's ability to transport its troops and supplies. This photograph depicts Sherman's men ripping up railroad tracks.

WILLIAM T. SHERMAN

A master of strategy, Sherman secured his reputation as a commander after his success at Vicksburg (see pages 96–97). His capture of Atlanta and ruthlessness on the "March to the Sea" tore apart the Confederacy and helped the Union win the War.

AT THE TIME, THE "MARCH" LEFT **$100 MILLION** WORTH OF DAMAGE IN ITS WAKE.

FACT FILE

LOCATIONS:
Atlanta and
Savannah, Georgia

DATE:
May 7–December 22, 1864

WHO WON:
Union

CASUALTIES: Union 33,000;
Confederacy 37,000

CONFEDERATE
COMMANDERS

Many graduates from the US Military Academy at West Point (see page 39) came from the South. A large number of them left the federal army to serve the Confederacy. Among the prominent Confederate military commanders were Robert E. Lee, Thomas Jackson, James Longstreet, and J. E. B. Stuart. Some of the other important ones are shown here.

ALBERT SIDNEY JOHNSTON
In command of the Confederate West, Johnston died of wounds suffered at Shiloh in April 1862.

JOSEPH EGGLESTON JOHNSTON
Johnston led Confederate forces from the First Battle of Bull Run in 1861 to the final surrender in 1865.

JOHN CLIFFORD PEMBERTON
An unsuccessful defense of Vicksburg in 1862–1863 was Pemberton's only significant action of the War.

BRAXTON BRAGG
Bragg resigned as commander of the Army of the Tennessee after his devastating defeat in the Battle of Chattanooga in November 1863.

AMBROSE POWELL HILL
Hill's successes at Antietam, Fredericksburg, and Chancellorsville were marred by later poor decisions, and he was killed at Petersburg in 1865.

JOHN BELL HOOD
An aggressive commander, Hood failed to stop Union General William T. Sherman during the 1864 Atlanta Campaign.

UNION COMMANDERS

The Union Army inherited the command structure of the prewar federal army, but it had just 18,000 soldiers and officers, with only four officers of general rank. Military leaders such as Ulysses S. Grant, David Farragut, George B. McClellan, and George H. Thomas drove the war effort. Some others who played a key role are listed here.

DAVID DIXON PORTER
Porter was in command of the Union Navy in the capture of New Orleans and Fort Fisher, and forced a fleet past the guns of Vicksburg.

JOSEPH HOOKER
"Fighting Joe" Hooker was replaced as commander of the Union Army of the Potomac after his disastrous defeat at Chancellorsville.

GEORGE GORDON MEADE
Meade replaced Hooker as commander of the Army of the Potomac and had his finest moment in his decisive victory at Gettysburg.

IRVIN MCDOWELL
McDowell survived defeat at the First Battle of Bull Run, only to be blamed for his role in the disaster at the Second Battle of Bull Run.

AMBROSE BURNSIDE
Although he was promoted after Antietam, Burnside suffered a disastrous defeat at Fredericksburg.

PHILIP HENRY SHERIDAN
Cavalry commander Sheridan's "scorched earth" tactics helped subdue the Shenandoah Valley in 1864.

CAUSE FOR CELEBRATION
In this engraving, a jubilant scene unfolds on the floor of the House of Representatives after it voted to pass the Thirteenth Amendment. Among those celebrating were African Americans watching from the public gallery.

THE THIRTEENTH
AMENDMENT

THE 1863 EMANCIPATION PROCLAMATION FREED ONLY SOME ENSLAVED PEOPLE AND NOT ALL.

Many feared slavery (see pages 18–19) might continue after the War. To prevent this, Lincoln proposed an amendment to the Constitution to outlaw slavery completely. Although the measure passed the Senate easily, Lincoln had far more difficulty persuading the House of Representatives to vote for it, which it eventually did in January 1865. It wasn't until December 6, when the Thirteenth Amendment became law, that slavery was finally abolished.

The original text of the Resolution proposing the Thirteenth Amendment

The Richmond Capitol, seat of the Confederate government ......

...... Residents and soldiers cross the Mayo Bridge across the James River.

THE FALL OF
RICHMOND

FLEEING THE FLAMES

Residents and Confederate soldiers stream across the James River as Richmond burns behind them on April 2, 1865. President Lincoln would visit the city two days later to inspect the now-captured Confederate capital.

IN 1865, TRAPPED BEHIND THE DEFENSES OF PETERSBURG, CONFEDERATE GENERAL ROBERT E. LEE'S PROSPECTS LOOKED GRIM.

One by one, Union General Grant (see page 56) cut off supply routes to Lee (see page 72), and the destruction of Pickett's division at Five Forks on April 1 made Lee's position hopeless. He evacuated Petersburg, leaving Richmond exposed. As panicked residents fled the next day, fires broke out. By the time the first Union forces entered the city on April 3, much of it was in ruins. Jefferson Davis (see page 29) and his government escaped by train to Danville, Virginia, and finally to Georgia, where he was arrested on May 10.

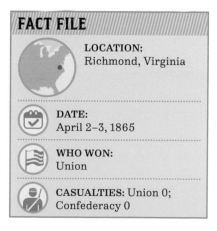

FACT FILE

LOCATION:
Richmond, Virginia

DATE:
April 2–3, 1865

WHO WON:
Union

CASUALTIES: Union 0;
Confederacy 0

Camp of 54th Mass Colored Regt.

1863

Morris Island. Dept of the South, Sept 28th

Your Excelency: Abraham Lincoln:

Your Excelency will perdon the presumtion of an humble individual like myself, in addressing you. but the earnest Solicitation of my Comrades in Arms. besides the genuine interest felt by myself in the matter is my excuse... before the Executive head of the Nation... and we can not supose him acting in any way interested. Now the main question is. Are we Soldiers, or are we Labourers. We are fully armed, and equipped, have done all the various Duties, pertaining to a Soldiers life, have conducted ourselves, to the complete satisfaction of General Officers, who were if any, prejudiced against us, but who now accord us all the encouragement, and honour due us: have shared the perils, and Labour, of Reducing the first stronghold, that flaunted a Traitor Flag: and more, Mr President. Today, the Anglo Saxon Mother, Wife, or Sister. are not alone, in tears for ...

EYEWITNESS: JAMES HENRY GOODING
AFRICAN AMERICAN SOLDIER

JAMES HENRY GOODING ASKED PRESIDENT LINCOLN FOR EQUAL PAY.

"Now the main question is are we soldiers, or are we labourers. We are fully armed, and equipped, have done all the various duties, pertaining to a soldier's life ...," he said, asking for the same wages as white soldiers.

A corporal in the 54th Massachusetts Regiment, he pointed out that African American soldiers performed the same duties as their white comrades but were paid only $10 a month, $3 less than them. The wages were finally made equal by Congress in 1864.

THE SOUTH SURRENDERS
Lee signed the surrender documents at a ceremony that took place in the house of the McLeans, a local family who moved from Bull Run after the first battle there to get away from the War.

LEE SURRENDERS AT
APPOMATTOX

General Ulysses S. Grant and his men look on as General Robert E. Lee surrenders.

AS HE WITHDREW FROM PETERSBURG, GENERAL ROBERT E. LEE HOPED TO JOIN THE LAST LARGE CONFEDERATE FORCE AT DANVILLE, VIRGINIA.

Badly needing supplies, he aimed for Amelia Court House, but found none there. Time wasted foraging allowed General Grant to catch up and destroy a quarter of Lee's force at Sayler's Creek. By April 9, 1865, the outnumbered Confederates were almost surrounded at Appomattox Court House. With no way out, Lee met with Grant at the McLean House and surrendered. After four years, the War was almost over.

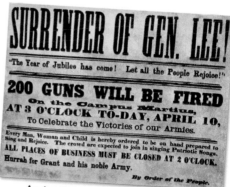

An April 10 poster announcing the surrender of General Lee and the celebration of the Confederacy's defeat

CIVIL WAR STAMPS

AS WELL AS DIVIDING THE NATION, THE WAR SPLIT THE POSTAL SERVICE IN TWO.

From August 1861, postal authorities in the North stopped delivering letters from the South and issued new stamps to stop the Confederacy from using the prewar ones. Around a third of post offices were in the South, and to serve these, the Confederacy issued its own stamps from October 1861. On both sides, mail played a vital role in keeping the morale of soldiers high with news from home.

15-cent stamp printed in black, in mourning for Abraham Lincoln in 1866

5-cent Confederate issue depicting President Jefferson Davis, printed in 1862, on plates imported from England

24-cent postage stamp showing Union General Winfield Scott, issued in 1870

10-cent Union stamp bearing the portrait of George Washington, issued in 1861

1-cent Benjamin Franklin stamp, part of the Union's reissue of stamps in August 1861

10-cent Thomas Jefferson stamp, the second-ever Confederate issue, printed in November 1861

2-cent New Orleans provisional stamp, issued before general Confederate stamps became available

THE ASSASSINATION OF
LINCOLN

PRESIDENT ABRAHAM LINCOLN LIVED ONLY A FEW DAYS AFTER ROBERT E. LEE'S SURRENDER.

There had been previous attacks on Lincoln—in 1864, his hat was shot off while riding alone—but the well-known actor and Confederate sympathizer John Wilkes Booth devised a new plot to kill the president. On April 14, 1865, Booth entered Lincoln's box at Ford's Theater in Washington, DC, and shot him in the head. Lincoln died early the next morning. Booth escaped, but was hunted down and shot on April 26.

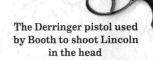

The Derringer pistol used by Booth to shoot Lincoln in the head

LINCOLN'S LAST ACT

The moment Booth shot Lincoln is depicted in this old engraving. As a well-known figure in the acting world, Booth found it easy to gain access to the theater and then the president's box.

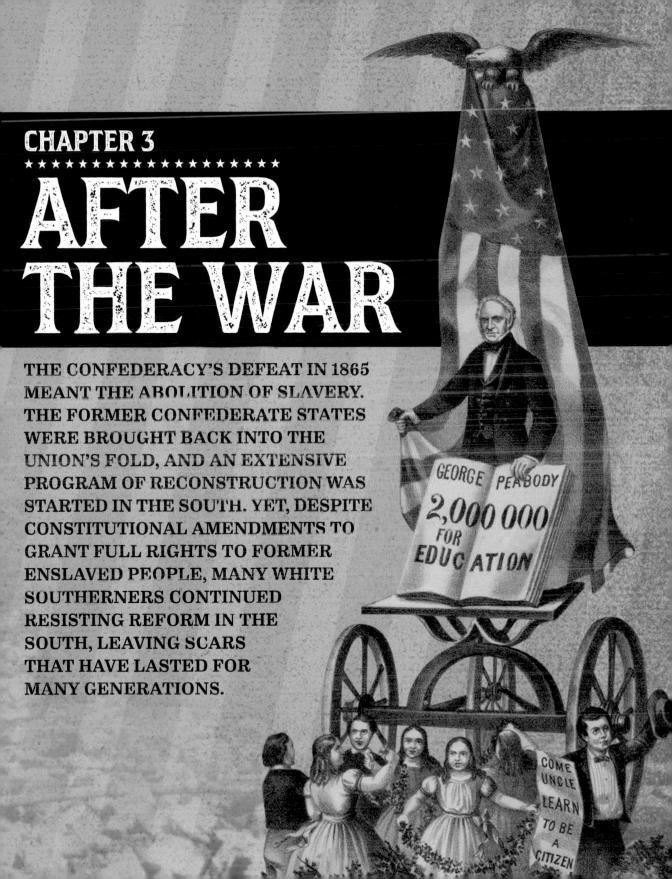

CHAPTER 3

★ ★ ★ ★ ★ ★ ★ ★ ★ ★ ★ ★ ★ ★ ★ ★ ★ ★

AFTER THE WAR

THE CONFEDERACY'S DEFEAT IN 1865
MEANT THE ABOLITION OF SLAVERY.
THE FORMER CONFEDERATE STATES
WERE BROUGHT BACK INTO THE
UNION'S FOLD, AND AN EXTENSIVE
PROGRAM OF RECONSTRUCTION WAS
STARTED IN THE SOUTH. YET, DESPITE
CONSTITUTIONAL AMENDMENTS TO
GRANT FULL RIGHTS TO FORMER
ENSLAVED PEOPLE, MANY WHITE
SOUTHERNERS CONTINUED
RESISTING REFORM IN THE
SOUTH, LEAVING SCARS
THAT HAVE LASTED FOR
MANY GENERATIONS.

THE AFTERMATH

ONCE THE WAR WAS OVER, HUGE CHALLENGES REMAINED. THE PHYSICAL DAMAGE HAD TO BE REPAIRED, WAR WOUNDED CARED FOR, AND FAMILIES REUNITED.

More than half a million soldiers had died, and in the South, half the agricultural machinery had been destroyed and hundreds of miles of railroad track torn up. The freedom granted to former enslaved African Americans had to be made real in the face of often still-hostile Southern white opinion, and the newly free needed means to support themselves economically. Measures had to be taken to bring the nation together. Politically, the former Confederate states underwent reforms to allow them to reenter the Union.

THE RESTORATION

In 1867–1868, Congress passed the Reconstruction Acts, requiring former Confederate states—now under military supervision—to abolish slavery and guarantee African American voting rights in order to be admitted back into the Union. Though the Union was restored, the Reconstruction plan did not change Southern attitudes and was considered a failure, as reflected in this cartoon from 1865.

Vice President Johnson tries hard to stitch the US back together.

THE STRUGGLES OF "FREEDOM"

Some Southern states passed "Black codes"—local laws restricting the rights of newly freed African Americans to work outside their former plantations. Once Reconstruction ended in 1877, Southern states enacted "Jim Crow" laws, making it hard for African Americans to vote, and enforcing segregation between whites and Blacks in education, housing, and employment. Seen above are the young students in an African American school in North Carolina.

A race riot breaks out in Charleston, South Carolina, in 1866.

SOUTHERN REACTION

Many white southerners resented the changes after the War, such as forcing voters to swear loyalty to the Constitution and the influence of "carpetbaggers," northerners who exploited the profits to be made in the South's rebuilding. There were many race riots (see above), and some people joined organizations such as the Ku Klux Klan, which engaged in violent attacks on African Americans.

TURBULENT POLITICS

Andrew Johnson, who became president after Lincoln's assassination, was impeached and nearly convicted in 1868, after Congress objected to his lenient policies toward the South. Seen above is a senator, who, despite being crippled by a stroke, came to cast his vote at Johnson's impeachment. "Redeemers"— radical southerners—gradually won back control of Southern state governments.

President Lincoln, who once worked as a rail splitter, uses a split rail to reposition the globe to help stitch it up.

FIGHTING DISCRIMINATION

Although the War did not achieve everything the victors hoped for, the Union had been preserved and slavery abolished, both big wins. However, the bitterness about the conflict and nostalgia for prewar Southern society left the South and North still divided. African Americans found their rights gradually removed, and it took another fight for Civil Rights to try to restore them. In 1963, a "March on Washington" was organized by leaders, including Martin Luther King Jr., to protest against racial discrimination.

A DEVASTATED CITY

Retreating Confederate troops set fires in Richmond (see page 133) to stop supplies from falling into Union hands. These got out of control and destroyed most of the city center.

WHITE SOUTHERNERS WHO **SUPPORTED** RECONSTRUCTION WERE INSULTINGLY CALLED SCALAWAGS.

❝ All persons born or naturalized in the United States ... are citizens of the United States. ❞

Section 1,
The Fourteenth Amendment,
US Constitution

Ruins of
Confederate
arsenal

Damaged
railroad
bridge

RESENTMENT IN THE SOUTH

The rebuilding in the South attracted many northerners who saw opportunities for quick profits. Many southerners resented this, accusing them of profiteering from the South's suffering and criticizing the development projects for former enslaved people that some of them funded. This picture shows the Northern financier George Peabody promising $2 million for schools for poor southerners.

THE SOUTH
IN RUINS

MORE THAN 600,000 SOLDIERS HAD DIED IN THE CIVIL WAR, THE SOUTH'S ECONOMY WAS IN RUINS, AND THE SOUTHERN STATES NEEDED REINTEGRATING INTO THE UNION.

War damage in the South meant a great deal of rebuilding was needed. A Reconstruction Act in 1867 appointed military governors to run the former Confederate states. They ensured that the states accepted the Fourteenth Amendment—which was passed in 1868 and guaranteed African American voting rights—before readmission to the Union. The process of Reconstruction allowed former enslaved people the opportunity to vote, and some African Americans gained political office. However, it was bitterly resented by many in the South, and soon, Democrat opponents, or "redeemers," began to take control of state legislatures to reverse the political gains won.

LIVING IN POVERTY
For many African Americans, the end of the War may have brought freedom, but they were left in desperate poverty. Here, a poor African American family of farmers is shown outside their North Carolina log cabin.

THE AFRICAN AMERICAN
STRUGGLE

FOLLOWING THE ABOLITION OF SLAVERY, FREED AFRICAN AMERICANS FACED MANY CHALLENGES.

The federal government set up the Freedmen's Bureau in 1865 to help educate and offer medical and economic assistance to newly freed African Americans, but many had to keep working on their former plantations as sharecroppers with little payment.

White supremacists also founded the Ku Klux Klan, a secret organization that violently opposed the granting of civil rights to African Americans. Once Reconstruction ended in 1877, Southern states passed laws enforcing segregation of white and Black people.

Ku Klux Klan members concealed their identities and spread terror.

MEMORIAL DAY

ON MAY 1, 1865, MORE THAN 10,000 PEOPLE PARADED IN CHARLESTON, SOUTH CAROLINA, TO HONOR THE CIVIL WAR DEAD.

Most of the people parading were freed African Americans. In the weeks leading up to the day, some of them had also helped reorganize the unmarked graves of fallen Union soldiers at a racetrack in the city. Elsewhere, people began to decorate the graves of fallen soldiers. These commemorations eventually evolved into a federal holiday called Memorial Day, when Americans killed in the Civil War and in other wars would be commemorated. In 1968, this holiday was moved to the last Monday of every May.

A DAY OF JUBILEE

Celebrated on June 19 every year, Juneteenth is the anniversary of Union General Gordon Granger's entry into Galveston, Texas, in 1865, where he declared the last enslaved people to be free. This illustration shows former enslaved people celebrating their "day of Jubilee".

SUMTER ONCE MORE

The Union flag is raised over Fort Sumter on April 14, 1865, in a ceremony to celebrate the end of the War. It was carried out by Union General Robert Anderson, the officer who had surrendered the fort four years previously.

EYEWITNESS: JOURDON ANDERSON
FORMERLY ENSLAVED

AS A FREE MAN, ANDERSON REPLIED TO HIS FORMER SLAVEHOLDER'S REQUEST THAT HE COME WORK FOR FREE.

"Although you shot at me twice before I left you, I did not want to hear of your being hurt, and am glad you are still living," Anderson wrote. He then sarcastically asked the slaveholder to pay him in back wages for his work while he was enslaved, writing, "At twenty-five dollars a month for me, and two dollars a week for Mandy, our earnings would amount to eleven thousand six hundred and eighty dollars." In pointing out a few uncomfortable truths, Anderson's letter is a rare document showing what former enslaved people really thought of those who had enslaved them. "Say howdy to George Carter, and thank him for taking the pistol from you when you were shooting at me," Anderson concluded.

Jourdon Anderson

Content of Anderson's letter as printed in a newspaper

Letter from a Freedman to his Old Master.

The following is a genuine document. It was dictated by the old servant, and contains his ideas and forms of expression. [Cincinnati Commercial.

DAYTON, Ohio, August 7, 1865.

To my Old Master, Col. P. H. ANDERSON, Big Spring, Tennessee.

SIR: I got your letter and was glad to find that you had not forgotten Jordan, and that you wanted me to come back and live with you again, promising to do better for me than anybody else can. I have often felt uneasy about you. I thought the Yankees would have hung you long before this for harboring Rebs. they found at your house. I suppose they never heard about your going to Col. Martin's to kill the Union soldier that was left by his company in their stable. Although you shot at me twice before I left you, I did not want to hear of your being hurt, and am glad you are still living. It would do me good to go back to the dear old home again and see Miss Mary and Miss Martha and Allen, Esther, Green and Lee. Give my love to them all, and tell them I hope we will meet in the better world, if not in this. I would have gone back to see you all when I was working in the Nashville Hospital, but one of the neighbors told me Henry intended to shoot me if he ever got a chance.

I want to know particularly what the good chance is you propose to give me. I am doing tolerably well here; I get $25 a month, with victuals and clothing; have a comfortable home for Mandy (the folks here call her Mrs. Anderson), and the children, Milly Jane and Grundy, go to school and are learning well; the teacher says Grundy has a head for a preacher. They go to Sunday-School, and Mandy and me attend church regularly. We are kindly treated; sometimes we overhear others saying, "Them colored people were slaves" down in Tennessee. The children feel hurt when they hear such remarks, but I tell them it was no disgrace in Tennessee to belong to Col. Anderson. Many darkies would have been proud, as I used to was, to call you master. Now, if you will write and say what wages you will give me, I will be better able to decide whether it would be to my advantage to move back again.

As to my freedom, which you say I can have, there is nothing to be gained on that score, as I got my free-papers in 1864 from the Provost-Marshal-General of the Department at Nashville. Mandy says she would be afraid to go back without some proof that you are sincerely disposed to treat us justly and kindly—and we have concluded to test your sincerity by asking you to send us our wages for the time we served you. This will make us forget and forgive old sores, and rely on your justice and friendship in the future. I served you faithfully for thirty-two years, and Mandy twenty years, at $25 a month for me, and $2 a week for Mandy. Our earnings would amount to $11,680. Add to this the interest for the time our wages has been kept back and deduct what you paid for our clothing and three doctor's visits to me, and pulling a tooth for Mandy, and the balance will show what we are in justice entitled to. Please send the money by Adams Express, in care of V. Winters, esq., Dayton, Ohio. If you fail to pay us for faithful labors in the past we can have little faith in your promises in the future. We trust the good Maker

CONSTITUTIONAL
AMENDMENTS

THE PRECIOUS VOTE

African American men line up to vote in
elections in Richmond, Virginia, in 1871.
After Reconstruction ended in 1877, many
Southern states passed laws making it hard
for African Americans to vote.

**THE THIRTEENTH AMENDMENT ABOLISHED
SLAVERY, BUT ENSURING THAT ALL FORMER
ENSLAVED PEOPLE ENJOYED FULL CIVIL
RIGHTS PROVED TO BE VERY DIFFICULT.**

In 1866, Congress passed the Fourteenth Amendment,
granting equal protection under the law to all Americans.
It stated that any state wanting readmission to the Union
had to accept it, but many in the South resisted, so
Congress passed a Fifteenth Amendment—ratified in
1870—declaring that nobody's right to vote would be
restricted on grounds of race.

> ❝ The right of citizens of
> the United States to vote
> shall not be denied ...
> on account of race, color,
> or previous condition
> of servitude. ❞
>
> Section 1, The Fifteenth
> Amendment, US Constitution

Party name

Justice,
blindfolded,
to show that her
decisions are fair

Ulysses S. Grant

NATIONAL UNION REPUBLICAN NOMINATION

FOR PRESIDENT,
Gen. U. S. GRANT
FOR VICE PRESIDENT,
SCHUYLER COLFAX

Schuyler
Colfax,
Grant's
running
mate

ELECT GRANT

The election poster for Grant's 1868 presidential campaign made much of symbols of American unity. The Bald Eagle on it reassured voters that the war hero would work to keep the Union safe.

GRANT ELECTED
PRESIDENT

WAR HERO ULYSSES S. GRANT WON A CONVINCING VICTORY FOR THE REPUBLICANS IN THE 1868 PRESIDENTIAL ELECTION.

However, the administration of President Grant (see page 56) was rocked by corruption scandals, and an economic depression turned Northern voters away from involvement in the South. Democrat "Redeemers" opposed to Reconstruction took power in most Southern states. When the 1876 election result was disputed, the Redeemers insisted on the end of Reconstruction.

GRANT'S **CAMPAIGN SLOGAN,** "LET US HAVE PEACE," WAS TAKEN FROM ONE OF HIS LETTERS.

HIRAM RHODES
REVELS

BORN FREE IN NORTH CAROLINA, REVELS BECAME A MINISTER AND, DURING THE CIVIL WAR, HE ORGANIZED AFRICAN AMERICAN REGIMENTS.

Revels also served as a Union Army chaplain. He made history in 1870 when he was elected as a senator for Mississippi, becoming the first African American man to achieve that distinction. He took the seat once held by former Confederate president Jefferson Davis (see page 29). Revels was joined in Washington, DC, the same year by Joseph James Rainey, the first African American man in the House of Representatives. Revels stepped down after a year to become president of Alcorn University, a historically Black institution.

❝ The people of the North owe to the colored race a deep obligation that is no easy matter to fulfill. ❞

Hiram Rhodes Revels, in a speech to the Senate, March 16, 1870

A SENATOR INSPIRES

This 1870 portrait of Revels by American artist Theodore Kauffman so impressed Frederick Douglass that he said it was a symbol of "the dividing line between the darkness and despair that overhung our past, and the light and hope that now beam upon our future."

CHAPTER 4

★★★★★★★★★★★★★★★★★★★★★★★★★★★★★★★★★

REFERENCE SECTION

THE CIVIL WAR WAS ONE OF THE MOST PIVOTAL PERIODS IN US HISTORY. THE FOLLOWING PAGES LIST SOME OF THE KEY BATTLES AND FACTS ABOUT THE FOUR-YEAR STRUGGLE THAT INVOLVED MORE THAN 3 MILLION SOLDIERS. ALSO FIND OUT ABOUT THE BATTLEFIELD PARKS, MEMORIALS, MUSEUMS, AND HISTORIC SITES THAT WILL HELP YOU LEARN MORE ABOUT THE WAR.

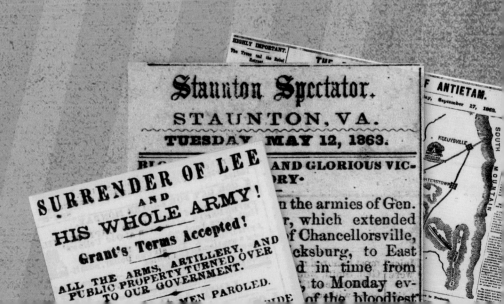

BATTLE FACTS

THE FOUR YEARS OF THE CIVIL WAR WERE SOME OF THE MOST MOMENTOUS YEARS IN AMERICAN HISTORY.

Listed here are some of the key statistics, important battles, and facts about the conflict that almost tore the United States apart.

NUMBER OF SOLDIERS

Union	2,128,948
Confederate	1,082,119

NUMBER OF DEATHS

Total	620,000
Due to disease	388,580

Source: American Battlefield Trust, 2020, and US National Park Service, 2020

BLOODIEST BATTLES

BATTLES	CASUALTIES
Gettysburg	51,112
Vicksburg	37,273
Chickamauga	34,624
Chancellorsville	30,764
The Wilderness	30,000
Spotsylvania Courthouse	30,000
Stones River	24,645
Shiloh	23,716
Antietam	22,717
Second Battle of Bull Run	22,177

Source: American Battlefield Trust, 2020

The first land battle—the First Battle of Bull Run—took place on Wilmer McLean's farm, from where he then moved out. Four years later, Lee surrendered in Wilmer's new house at Appomattox Court House. McLean was quoted as saying, "The War began in my front yard and ended in my front parlor."

Francis Miles Finch wrote the poem *The Blue and the Gray* to honor the dead of both sides.

After the Battle of Shiloh, many of the 16,000 injured soldiers reported their wounds glowed in the dark. This was caused by a type of bacteria that reacts with light.

John Wilkes Booth's brother Edwin saved Lincoln's son, Robert, when he fell on a railroad track in 1864.

OTHER KEY BATTLES

From 1861 to 1865, there were more than 10,500 military engagements, from minor skirmishes to huge field battles. This book covers some of the most important battles, but listed here are some more.

The Battle of Philippi	June 3, 1861
The Battle of Wilson's Creek	August 10, 1861
The Battle of Hatteras Inlet	August 28–29, 1861
The Battle of Ball's Bluff	October 21, 1861
The Battle of Belmont	November 7, 1861
The Battle of Mill Springs	January 19, 1862
The First Battle of Kernstown	March 23, 1862
The Battle of Seven Pines	May 31–June 1, 1862
The First Battle of Memphis	June 6, 1862
The Battle of Gaines' Mill	June 27, 1862
The Battle of Malvern Hill	July 1, 1862
The Battle of Cedar Mountain	August 9, 1862
The Battle of South Mountain	September 14, 1862
The First Battle of Sabine Pass	September 24–25, 1862
The Second Battle of Corinth	October 3–4, 1862
The Battle of Perryville	October 8, 1862
The Battle of Arkansas Post	January 9–11, 1863
The Siege of Port Hudson	May 21–July 9, 1863
The Battle of Brandy Station	June 9, 1863
The Battle of Resaca	May 13–15, 1864
The Battle of New Market	May 15, 1864
The Battle of Peachtree Creek	July 20, 1864
The Battle of Globe Tavern	August 18–21, 1864
The Battle of Waynesboro	December 4, 1864
The Battle of Bentonville	March 19–21, 1865
The Battle of Sayler's Creek	April 6, 1865
The Battle of Palmito Ranch	May 12–13, 1865

At 106, Albert Woolson became the last Civil War veteran to die, in 1956. He was once a Union Army drummer boy.

More than 1,500 Medals of Honor were awarded by Congress during the War—all to Union soldiers.

During the War, the Union captured 462,634 Confederate soldiers, of whom 25,976 died in prison.

The oldest soldier to serve in the Civil War was 80-year-old Union soldier Curtis King from Iowa.

More American soldiers died in the Civil War than in the two World Wars combined.

REMEMBERING
THE WAR

THE CIVIL WAR HAS A CENTRAL PLACE IN THE HISTORY OF THE US.

It is remembered in numerous places throughout the country—the battlefields, houses, museums, and cemeteries—all of which bear witness to a conflict that cost millions of lives.

MEMORIALS

Memorials of the War commemorate the conflict and the lives touched by it. The states in which the War was fought are dotted with monuments to the War's leading figures. Most Civil War soldiers were buried near where they fell—many of them never identified—and their resting places are in cemeteries close to battlefields or major garrison centers.

THE MCLEAN HOUSE
Appomattox, Virginia
The local farmer's house where Grant and Lee negotiated the surrender of the Confederate Army of Northern Virginia has been preserved as it was.

THE STONEWALL JACKSON HOUSE
Lexington, Virginia
The restored house of Confederate General Thomas "Stonewall" Jackson contains period furniture and many of his personal possessions.

AFRICAN AMERICAN CIVIL WAR MEMORIAL AND MUSEUM
Washington, DC
The memorial remembers the contribution of the 200,000 African Americans who fought in the Union's Armed Forces (Army and Navy).

GENERAL GRANT NATIONAL MEMORIAL
New York City, New York
The tomb of the Union Army's most successful general serves as a memorial to his life and achievements, both as general and president.

LINCOLN MEMORIAL
Washington, DC
This iconic memorial honors the 16th president and his role in defending the Union and achieving the abolition of slavery.

WHITNEY PLANTATION
Wallace, Louisiana
This museum tells the story of the enslaved people on a former sugar plantation.

ARLINGTON NATIONAL CEMETERY
Arlington, Virginia
On the grounds of Robert E. Lee's former mansion, the cemetery contains military dead from all of the United States' wars. Burials began during the Civil War, starting in Lee's front yard.

ANTIETAM NATIONAL CEMETERY
Sharpsburg, Maryland
The cemetery was established in 1865 to give proper burials to the soldiers who died in the country's single bloodiest day of battle.

CHATTANOOGA NATIONAL CEMETERY
Chattanooga, Tennessee
The burial ground contains the remains of 44,000 soldiers, most of whom died in the Civil War battles at Chickamauga and Chattanooga.

GETTYSBURG NATIONAL CEMETERY
Gettysburg, Pennsylvania
This is the resting place of more than 3,500 Union soldiers who fell in the battle. Its dedication inspired Lincoln to give the Gettysburg Address.

NATIONAL PARKS

The National Park Service and other groups preserve and remember battlefields and other large sites associated with the Civil War.

FREDERICKSBURG AND SPOTSYLVANIA NATIONAL MILITARY PARK
Fredericksburg, Virginia
The world's largest military park covers an area in which four major Civil War battles were fought between 1862 and 1865.

GETTYSBURG NATIONAL MILITARY PARK
Gettysburg, Pennsylvania
Preserving the site of the largest battle fought in North America, the park contains statues and monuments (see left) to many individuals and units.

MANASSAS NATIONAL BATTLEFIELD PARK
Prince William County, Virginia
The park preserves the site of the two battles at Bull Run (Manassas), including monuments and houses such as Stone House, used as a hospital in both battles.

SHILOH NATIONAL MILITARY PARK
Shiloh, Tennessee
On the site of the largest battle of the Mississippi River Valley, the park includes an interpretative center that also covers the Siege and the Battle of Corinth.

REENACTMENTS

Thousands of reenactors don authentic Confederate and Union uniforms, with replicas of weapons, to recreate the biggest battles of the Civil War. These reenactments serve to educate people about the War.

MUSEUMS

Many specialist museums hold items associated with the Civil War: uniforms; weapons; and personal items such as diaries, which tell the stories of people who took part in the struggle, both on the battlefield and at home.

AMERICAN CIVIL WAR MUSEUM
Richmond, Virginia
With sites including the Confederate White House, the museum concentrates on the Confederacy's side of the War.

ATLANTA HISTORY CENTER
Atlanta, Georgia
With one of the country's largest Civil War collections, this museum (see above) contains uniforms, cannons, and a 358-ft (109-m) long panoramic painting of the Battle of Atlanta.

HAMPTON ROADS NAVAL MUSEUM
Norfolk, Virginia
Covering the long history of the US Navy, the museum's Civil War collection includes items from the Confederate ironclad CSS *Virginia*.

NATIONAL CIVIL WAR MUSEUM
Harrisburg, Pennsylvania
This building houses more than 20,000 artifacts, documents, and photographs from both sides of the Civil War.

NATIONAL PRISONER OF WAR MUSEUM
Andersonville, Georgia
A museum on the site of the largest Confederate prison camp, which held more than 45,000 Union prisoners of war (POWs), this covers the experience of US POWs in the Civil War and other conflicts.

THE NATIONAL MUSEUM OF AMERICAN HISTORY
Washington, DC
Part of the Smithsonian Institution, this one contains an extensive collection of Civil War artifacts, including the hat Lincoln wore the night the president was assassinated.

GLOSSARY

ABOLITIONIST
A person who called for the abolition (ending) of slavery in the US.

ACT
A law passed by Congress that has come into effect.

AMENDMENT
A change in the constitution of a country. In the US, it must be passed by Congress to come into effect.

AMPUTATION
The cutting off of a body part by a surgeon.

ANESTHETIC
A medical substance that makes a patient unable to feel pain during a surgical procedure.

ARMY CORPS
An army unit made up of two or more divisions (units that held up to 12,000 soldiers each).

ARTILLERY
Mortars, cannons, or other large guns that can shoot over long distances.

BAYONET
A metal blade with a sharp point attached to the end of a musket for use in hand-to-hand combat.

BORDER STATES
Union States that allowed slavery but did not break away from the Union. These were Delaware, Kentucky, Maryland, Missouri, and West Virginia.

BOUNTY
A bonus paid as an enticement to men for enlisting in the army.

CAMPAIGN
A series of military movements by an army in an area during a war.

CASUALTIES
The number of dead, wounded, or captured soldiers in a battle.

CAVALRY
Soldiers who fought on horseback.

CIVIL WAR
The War between the Union and the Confederate States of America from 1861–1865.

CONFEDERACY
The 11 states that broke off from the Union to form the independent country of the Confederate States of America in 1861. This was folded back into the United States at the end of the War.

CONGRESS
The government body in the United States that makes laws.

CONSCRIPTION
Compulsory enlistment in the Armed Forces. This was done by both sides during the Civil War.

CONTRABAND
A term used for enslaved people who escaped from the Confederacy.

COTTON GIN
A machine used to separate the seeds from the harvested cotton plant. It was invented by American engineer Eli Whitney.

DESERTION
Leaving a military unit without permission. This was an offense that was punishable by death during the Civil War.

EMANCIPATION PROCLAMATION
A proclamation by President Abraham Lincoln on January 1, 1863, that declared all African American enslaved people in the Confederacy to be free.

ENSLAVED PEOPLE
African Americans sold into enslavement under white slaveholders. *See* slavery.

ENTRENCHMENTS
A system of trenches and other defenses on a battlefield.

FEDERAL ARMORY
A facility where the US government stores weapons and ammunition.

FLANK
Extreme edges of an army unit's lines. Also to send army units around the edges of the enemy's army.

FLOTILLA
A group of naval vessels smaller than a fleet.

FUGITIVE SLAVE ACTS
A pair of US federal laws in the 18th and 19th centuries that demanded the return of enslaved people to their slaveholders in the South.

GARRISON
A group of soldiers defending a fort, town, or city.

GUNBOAT
A small, fast ship armed with guns used for defense along coastlines or on rivers.

INDUSTRIAL REVOLUTION
A period in the 18th and 19th centuries when the invention of new machines caused industry to grow quickly.

INFANTRY
Soldiers who fight on foot.

IRONCLAD
A warship during the Civil War that was protected by heavy iron plates as a defense against enemy fire.

KU KLUX KLAN
A secret group of white people that violently opposed the granting of civil rights to former enslaved African Americans after the War.

MEXICAN-AMERICAN WAR
A conflict between the United States and Mexico in 1846–1848, after the US took over the state of Texas, previously owned by Mexico.

MILITIA
Citizen-soldiers who are not part of an official army.

MINIÉ BALL
A muzzle-loaded lead bullet used by Civil War soldiers in their rifled muskets.

MUSKET
A gun with a barrel that is long and smooth inside, unlike a rifle. See rifle.

PLANTATIONS
Large estates (mainly in the Southern US) on which crops, such as cotton, were grown, often cultivated by enslaved African American people.

PRISONER OF WAR
A soldier captured by the enemy in battle and held prisoner by them.

PRIVATEER
A civilian person, or ship, given permission by the government to attack enemy ships.

RAIDERS
A small group of soldiers that attack behind enemy lines.

RECONCILIATION
A movement that tried to reconcile the North and South after the Civil War, often by ignoring the slavery issue and instead remembering the War as a conflict between the white northerners and southerners.

RECONSTRUCTION
A period of political reform in the South from 1865–1877, during which the former Confederate states were placed under military supervision by the US government, before being let back into the Union.

REDEEMER
Southern politician who wanted to end Reconstruction.

REGIMENT
A unit in an army of around 2,000 soldiers, made up of many battalions (units with 300 or more soldiers).

RIFLE
A gun with a grooved barrel that shoots farther and more accurately than a musket. See musket.

SCOUT
Soldier who goes ahead of his main army unit to find information about the terrain and location of the enemy.

SECESSION
The act of withdrawing part of the country from the control of the country's government, as done by 11 Southern states in 1861 and 1862.

SLAVE POWER
A term used in the US to denote the political power and influence of slaveholders and their white supporters.

SLAVERY
The system of owning people as property with no rights, as well as having people work with no pay.

TARIFF
A tax or duty that must be paid on goods imported from or exported to a country.

THEATER
Large area in which parts of a war take place.

TORPEDO
An explosive device used in water that explodes on contact with a ship. Used by the navies in the Civil War.

TRIAGE
A process to decide the order in which patients or battlefield casualties should be treated, depending on the severity of wounds. In the US, it began in field hospitals in the Civil War.

UNDERGROUND RAILROAD
A network of people and safe houses established in the US in the 19th century by sympathetic antislavers to smuggle escaped enslaved people to the Northern free states or to Canada.

UNION
The 25 states (20 free states and 5 border states) that did not break away and remained part of the US during the Civil War from 1861–1865.

UNITED STATES COLORED TROOPS
Units in the Union Army formed from African American volunteers, mostly after the Emancipation Proclamation in 1863.

UNITED STATES SANITARY COMMISSION
An organization of civilians that gave medical and hygiene advice, as well as supplies, to Union soldiers during the Civil War.

VETERAN
A soldier who has fought in a previous war. Veterans fighting the Civil War had fought in the War of 1812 against Britain and in the Mexican-American War (1846–1848).

WEST POINT MILITARY ACADEMY
The military school in New York State that has trained US Army cadets since 1802, and from which many Civil War generals graduated, including Generals Grant, McClellan, and Lee.

INDEX
• • • • • • • • • • • • • • • • • • •

Page numbers in **bold** refer to main entries.

ACKNOWLEDGMENTS

The publisher would like to thank the following people for their help with making the book: Parnika Bagla, Shatarupa Chaudhuri, Virien Chopra, Upamanyu Das, Nayan Keshan, Bipasha Roy, and Manjari Thakur for editorial assistance; Mansi Agrawal, Sifat Fatima, and Baibhav Parida for design assistance; Deepak Negi and Vagisha Pushp for picture research assistance; Jaypal Singh, Bimlesh Tiwary, and Tanveer Zaidi for DTP assistance; Rakesh Kumar, Priyanka Sharma, and Saloni Singh for the jacket; Caroline Stamps for anglicizing and proofreading; and Helen Peters for the index.

Smithsonian Enterprises:

Kealy Gordon, Product Development Manager; Jill Corcoran, Director, Licensed Publishing; Janet Archer, DMM, Ecom and D-to-C; Carol LeBlanc, President

The publisher would like to thank the following for their kind permission to reproduce their photographs:

(Key: a-above; b-below/bottom; c-center; f-far; l-left; r-right; t-top)

123RF.com: Roystudio 4-155 (Background texture); **akg-images:** Glasshouse / Circa Images 139r, 142bc; **Alamy Stock Photo:** Alpha Stock 100crb, 100bl, Archive Pics 129tl, BC Photo 154tr, Chronicle 14–15, 120, Classic Image 16–17, Ian Dagnall 43, Randy Duchaine 26–27, Everett Collection Historical 11tl, 15tr, 20crb, 33, 54, 141crb, 144t, Everett Collection Inc. 46–47, 130crb, 155crb, 144crb, FLHC25 117crb, Gado Images / Sheridan Libraries / Levy 71ca, Gado Images / Smith Collection 13tr, Granger Historical Picture Archive 4tl, 9tr, 10–11, 24, 28, 71cla, 73, 87tr, 98–99, 103, 112tr, 112c, 114br, 122crb, 140clb, 141tl, The Granger Collection 23, 118tr, 141tr, Heritage Image Partnership Ltd. 133, Historic Collection 123crb, Historic Images 110cl, History and Art Collection 70r, 122cb, Incamerastock 137, Interfoto / History 59cb, Eric James 155tr, John Frost Newspapers 106cr, Lebrecht Music & Arts 37tr, 61, 65clb, National Geographic Image Collection / Tom Lovell 135t, Niday Picture Library 41, 53, 66, 92–93, 121, North Wind Picture Archives 12clb, 25, 31, 40cl, 40bl, 52, 68–69, 75, 89, 104, 114t, 132t, 138bl, 147, nsf 123cr, Old Paper Studios 108, Photo12 / Archives Snark 22tr, Pictorial Press Ltd. 2, 34–35, 96tr, 113, 123c, 131crb, 149l, The Picture Art Collection 17tl, Pictures Now 47crb, Chris Pondy 59crb, The Protected Art Archive 145, Roman Numeral Photographs 64r, Maurice Savage 94tr, Science History Images 38t, 119t, 136cl, Virginia Museum of History & Culture 70bl, 123cl; **Andy Thomas Fine Art:** 88; **Bridgeman Images:** 40c, © Civil War Archive 50cl, 50c, 50clb, 50bl, 51r, 58–59c, 58–59cb, 59ca, 59c, 71cra, © Don Troiani 3, 50cb, 50bc, 50r, 51ca, 51clb, 51bl, 51bc, 71cr, 71crb, 84cl, 84c, 84bc,

84–85t, 84–85b, 85tr, 94cra, 94clb, 94cb, 94br, 109crb, Estate of Josiah K. Lilly 115crb, 115crb (Liberty Head), Peter Newark Military Pictures 122cl, Photo © Don Troiani 40bc, PVDE 30, The Stapleton Collection 126, Don Troiani 4tr, 5tr, 35, 42, 76–77, 109t, 127, 150–151, David H. Wright 72; **Digital image courtesy of the Getty's Open Content Program:** Timothy H. O'Sullivan 18–19; **Dorling Kindersley:** Board of Trustees of the Royal Armouries 58cb, Gettysburg National Military Park 84bl, 84–85cb, 85cra, 85cr, 85cb, 85crb, 85crb (Amputation knife), 85b, Gettysburg National Military Park, PA 94cla, Jacob Termansen / Pia Marie Molbech / Peter Keim 40cr; **Dreamstime.com:** Chaoss 152–153 (Paper texture), Designprintck 6–7 (Background texture), Erik Lattwein 9cr; **Getty Images:** Bettmann 15tl, Bettmann / Contributor 65r, Buyenlarge / Contributor / Archive Photos 55, William F. Campbell / Contributor 20 (All photo frames), 90tr, 90clb, 90bl, 111 (All photo frames), 122–123 (All photo frames), Tria Giovan / Contributor / Corbis Historical 122cr, Tria Giovan / Corbis Documentary 104cra, Historical / Contributor / Corbis Historical 5tl, 62, 62–63, 78, 80t, 119cr, 138–139, 142–143, Kean Collection / Staff / Archive Photos 96–97, Layne Kennedy / The Image Bank Unreleased 26, MPI / Stringer / Archive Photos 148, Stock Montage / Contributor / Archive Photos 56, Time Life Pictures / The LIFE Picture Collection 45, Ullstein Bild Dtl. / Contributor 49; **Getty Images / iStock:** Bazzier 36–37; **Heritage Auctions, HA.com:** 90br, 90r, 115clb; **hmdb. org:** Photograph © J. J. Prats / Original-National Tribune Jun. 22, 1914" artist Klapp. 125t; **The Huntington- Library, Art Museum, and Botanical Gardens:** 21bl; **Library of Congress, Washington, DC:** 106cb, 106crb, 122clb, 146r, 151br, ca07003337 74bl, E668 .D55 74cl, LC USZ62-23098 101tl, LC USZ62-86078 101cl, LC USZ62-86080 100cl, LC-B811-2665 111br, LC-B811-4016 111bl, LC-BH82- 2417 29, LC-DIG cwpb-01826 48–49, LC-DIG cwpb-03950 37bl, LC-DIG ds-07220 123cb, LC-DIG pga-02601 8tr, LC-DIG pga-03035 37crb, LC-DIG pga-06141 36clb, LC-DIG ppmsca- 46394 9c, LC-DIG ppmsca-11274 101br, LC-DIG ppmsca-31540 13c, LC-DIG ppmsca-34764 71clb, LC-DIG ppmsca-35124 36br, LC-DIG ppmsca-36454 111tl, LC-DIG ppmsca-57689 / M. H. Kimball 12r, LC-DIG- ppmsca-30978 81, LC-DIG-cwpb-00741 152-153, LC-DIG-cwpb-01286 124, LC-DIG-cwpb-01550 117, LC-DIG-cwpb-03119 60crb, LC-DIG-cwpb-03356 128–129, LC-DIG-cwpb-03518 111cr, LC-DIG-cwpb-03769 82, LC-DIG-cwpb-04806 131cl, LC-DIG-cwpb-06280 130c, LC-DIG-cwpb-07427 130clb, LC-DIG-cwpb-07469 130cl, LC-DIG-cwpb-07587 122c, LC-DIG-cwpb-00463 130cb, LC-DIG-cwpbh-00839 131c, LC-DIG-cwpbh-01069 107, LC-DIG-cwpbh-01198 131cr, LC-DIG-ds-01484 125cr, LC-DIG-ds-05099 91, LC-DIG-highsm-04711

137cra, LC-DIG-highsm-06741 155bl, LC-DIG-pga-01846 105, LC-DIG-pga-01851 86, LC-DIG-pga-02797 79b, LC-DIG-pga-02817 13br, LC-DIG-pga-02834 40br, LC-DIG-pga-06201 60t, LC-DIG-pga-07513 116tr, LC-DIG-ppmsca-10978 145tr, LC-DIG-ppmsca-17158 140–141, LC-DIG-ppmsca-33091 67, LC-DIG-ppmsca-33767 118b, LC-DIG-ppmsca-38007 69tr, LC-DIG-ppmsca-40543 131cb, LC-DIG-ppmsca-52069 20cl, LC-DIG-ppmsca-53260 20cr, LC-DIG-ppmsca-58269 20cb, LC-DIG-ppmsca-67943 64bl, LC-DIG-stereo-1s01796 83, LC-DIG-USZ62-105530 19br, LC-USZ62-108564 80br, LC-USZ62-130838 130cr, LC-USZ62-99877 123clb, mfd.51002 21cr, ms000001.mss30189a.1845200 116clb, 116bl, ms000001.mss30189a.1862600 116crb, sn83030313 106cl, 151fbr, sn83045462 106clb, 151bc, sn84026366 31tr; **Mary Evans Picture Library:** Iberfoto 22c; **The Metropolitan Museum of Art, New York:** The Crosby Brown Collection of Musical Instruments, 1889 71b, Gilman Collection, Museum Purchase, 2005 95; **Missouri Historical Society, St. Louis:** 44tr; courtesy of the **National Park Service:** 21br; **National Museum of American History / Smithsonian Institution:** 115cra, 115br; **National Portrait Gallery, Smithsonian Institution:** 20c, Gift of Larry J. West 111tr; **Naval History and Heritage Command:** 57; **The New York Public Library:** 76cla, Gustavus W. Pach 39; **Houghton Library, Harvard University:** MS Am 1910 (14) 102t, MS Am 1910. Gift of Mrs. Lloyd K. Garrison, Mrs. Alexander D. Harvey, Frances Jay, and Mrs. Lawrence Fox, 1975 102cl, Portrait File (Shaw, Robert Gould) 102crb; **Rex by Shutterstock:** Granger 11br, 13cla; Courtesy of **Smithsonian. ©2020 Smithsonian:** 1951-93-4 / Gift of Arthur B. Carlson 32, 136c, National Museum of American History 58bc, 58–59t, 58–59b, 59cla, 71cb, 101tr, 101bl, 110cb, 110br, National Portrait Gallery 20clb, 131clb, National Postal Museum 136cra, 136bl, 136bc, 136br, 136fbr, NPG.74.75 / National Portrait Gallery 21tr; **South Caroliniana Library:** 87bl; **The US National Archives and Records Administration:** 134 (both images), Brady National Photographic Art Gallery (Washington, DC) 111cl, Mathew Brady 38crb, General Records of the United States Government; Record Group 11 132crb; **Wikipedia:** 74br, 146bl; **The Wilson Library, University of North Carolina at Chapel Hill:** 44b, 74cr, Documenting the American South 115cla, 115bl, E 449 D746 1845 / Documenting the American South 74bc, E487 .C52 87r, E608 .B78 v.1 1865 / Documenting the American South 74c

All other images © Dorling Kindersley
For further information see:
www.dkimages.com